HESSIAN CHAPLAINS

Their Diaries and Duties

Compiled and Translated by
Bruce E. Burgoyne

With Special Assistance from His Wife
Marie E. Burgoyne

HERITAGE BOOKS
2020

HERITAGE BOOKS
AN IMPRINT OF HERITAGE BOOKS, INC.

Books, CDs, and more—Worldwide

For our listing of thousands of titles see our website
at
www.HeritageBooks.com

Published 2020 by
HERITAGE BOOKS, INC.
Publishing Division
5810 Ruatan Street
Berwyn Heights, Md. 20740

Copyright © 2003 Bruce E. Burgoyne

All rights reserved. No part of this book may be reproduced or transmitted in any form or by any means, electronic or mechanical, including photocopying, recording or by any information storage and retrieval system without written permission from the author, except for the inclusion of brief quotations in a review.

International Standard Book Number
Paperbound: 978-0-7884-2359-8

Contents

Preface   i

Introduction   v

Church Book of
Hesse-Cassel Chaplain
Georg C. Coester   1

Chaplain Braunsdorf's
Anhalt-Zerbst
Church Book   61

Ansbach-Bayreuth
Church Book
Compiled by
Chaplain Stroelein   132

Heritage Books by Bruce E. Burgoyne:

*Aboard a Dutch Troop Transport: A Diary Written by
Captain Ludwig Alberti of the Waldeck 5th Battalion*

*A Hessian Officer's Diary of the American Revolution
Translated from an Anonymous Ansbach-Bayreuth Diary and the Prechtel Diary*

*Canada During the American Revolutionary War: Lieutenant Friedrich Julius von Papet's
Journal of the Sea Voyage to North America and the Campaign Conducted There*

CD: A Hessian Diary of the American Revolution

CD: A Hessian Officer's Diary of The American Revolution

*CD: A Hessian Report on the People, the Land, the War of Eighteenth Century
America, as Noted in the Diary of Chaplain Philipp Waldeck, 1776–1780*

CD: Ansbach-Bayreuth Diaries from the Revolutionary War

CD: Canada During the America Revolutionary War

CD: Diaries of Two Ansbach Jaegers

CD: The Hessian Collection, Volume 1: Revolutionary War Era

CD: They Also Served. Women with the Hessian Auxiliaries

CD: Waldeck Soldiers of the American Revolutionary War

Defeat, Disaster, and Dedication

Diaries of Two Ansbach Jaegers

*Eighteenth Century America (A Hessian Report on the People, the Land, the War)
as Noted in the Diary of Chaplain Philipp Waldeck (1776–1780)*

Enemy Views: The American Revolutionary War as Recorded by the Hessian Participants

*English Army and Navy Lists Compiled During the American Revolutionary War by
Ansbach-Bayreuth Lieutenant Johann Ernst Prechtel*

*Georg Pausch's Journal and Reports of the Campaign in America, as
Translated from the German Manuscript in the Lidgerwood Collection in the
Morristown Historical Park Archives, Morristown, New Jersey*

*Hesse-Hanau Order Books, a Diary and Roster: A Collection of Items
Concerning the Hesse-Hanau Contingent of "Hessians" Fighting
Against the American Colonists in the Revolutionary War*

Hessian Chaplains: Their Diaries and Duties

Hessian Letters and Journals and a Memoir

Journal of a Hessian Grenadier Battalion

Journal of the Hesse-Cassel Jaeger Corps

Journal of the Prince Charles Regiment
Translated by Bruce E. Burgoyne; Edited by Dr. Marie E. Burgoyne

*Most Illustrious Hereditary Prince: Letters to Their Prince
from Members of Hesse-Hanau Military Contingent in the
Service of England During the American Revolution*

Notes from a British Museum

Order Book of the Hesse-Cassel von Mirbach Regiment

*Revolutionary War Letters Written by Hessian Officers:
Generals Wilhelm von Knyphausen, Carl Wilhelm Von Hachenberg,
Friedrich Wilhelm von Lossberg, Johann Friedrich Cochenhausen,
Friedrich Von Riedesel and Major Carl Leopold von Baurmeister*
Bruce E. Burgoyne and Dr. Marie E. Burgoyne

The Diary of Lieutenant von Bardeleben and Other von Donop Regiment

The Hesse-Cassel Mirbach Regiment in the American Revolution

These Were the Hessians

The Third English-Waldeck Regiment in the American Revolutionary War

*The Trenton Commanders: Johann Gottlieb Rall and
George Washington, as Noted in Hessian Diaries*

Waldeck Soldiers of the American Revolutionary War

PREFACE

PREFACE

Over the years, I have translated a number of documents dealing with the diaries and duties of chaplains, serving with the so-called *Hessians,* who came to America as English auxiliaries, to suppress the revolt in the American colonies.

Two of the larger documents have been published as: *Eighteenth Century America,* Heritage Books, Inc. (Bowie, MD, 1995), the diary of Chaplain Philipp Waldeck of the Waldeck Regiment; and *Diaries of a Hessian Chaplain and the Chaplain's Assistant,* published by the Pfaltzgraff Pottery Company, (York, PA, 1990), for the Johannes Schwalm Historical Association, Inc., which is the diary of Chaplain Heinrich Kuemmell and Private Valentin Asteroth, both of the Hesse-Cassel von Huyne Regiment.

These two documents, plus the documents in this volume, present an interesting and different picture of the Hessians, which will give the reader a more sympathetic understanding of the men who came to America as enemies, but many of whom helped our American ancestors in the struggle for independence.

Although six German states contributed military units to the English effort, three are noted here, and the fourth, Waldeck, is covered by *Eighteenth Century*

America.

The material concerning Chaplain Coester, of Hesse-Cassel, was translated from *Geschichliches Nachrichten aus Treysa*, 1916, the German text of which is in the Evangelical Parsonage, Malsfeld, Hesse. (Inventar IIS, 68/69A.c. Nr. 28)

. The items about, and in part, by Chaplain Johann Gottlieb Siegismund Braunsdorf, include my translation of his church book, the original of which is in the Evangelical-Lutheran Church Archives in Jever, Germany; and an article, *An Anhalt Military Church Book in Jever* by Brigitte Heenicke and Gerorg Jahn, which appeared in the *Norddeutsche Familiekunde*, for January through March 1986.

The final portion of this volume is a church book compiled by Pastor Gregorius Michael Stroelein, the original which is in the Landeskirchliche Archiv, Zentrale Kirchebuchstelle, Am Oelberg 2, 8400 Regensburg, Germany.

It has been my pleasure, working and traveling with my wife, to bring the information contained in this volume to my readers. I hope, after they have read and considered the content, that they will have a deeper, more sympathetic understanding of the men who fought on both sides in the American Revolutionary War.

I thank all those individuals who have located and provided me with the German texts, Heritage Books, Inc. for many years of publishing my translations, and my patient wife, Marie, who has put up with my wandering into the past.

Bruce E. Burgoyne
September 2002
Dover, De.

INTRODUCTION

HESSIAN CHAPLAINS

INTRODUCTION

The care for the souls of Hesse-Cassel soldiers in the second half of the 18th Century was entrusted to the community pastors of specific troop localities. Special garrison jurisdictions in 1776 were only in Cassel, which had two garrison chaplains, in Marburg, which had one, and in Rinteln, where the pastor for the Reformed parish of the city, was responsible for the duties of garrison chaplain.

These four troop chaplains naturally were not sufficient for the troops scattered about in the field. Furthermore, the respective clergy were already too old for strenuous field service.

Therefore, it was necessary to acquire special chaplains, as had been done in six previous wars in which Hesse-Cassel participated.

The treaty, according to which Landgrave Friedrich II of Hesse-Cassel placed an auxiliary corps at the disposal of King George III of England, was signed on 15 January 1776. The preliminary negotiations had continued for a long time, so there was sufficient time and opportunity to recruit young theologians and chaplains for that war. Almost all had only recently left the university (Only Virnau was already a rector in Felsberg, and Becker was pastor in St. Goarshausen.) , and earned their keep as tutors or in similar situations.

The chaplains were considered as military personnel. No special dress was prescribed for their position. As the robe was officially introduced into the church only in 1835, they wore civilian dress, adopted to their position - a cap or hat, a coat, which according to the custom of the time, was cut somewhat similar to our frock coat. Because they were mounted, when making long marches with the troops, they may have worn boots. For their horses, they received a special forage allowance. Their pay amounted to 22 Thalers, 6 Albus (about 100 1969 Deutschmarks), and 18 Thalers expense money (per diem) for themselves and their servant. They also received an officers share in the distribution of booty. They were also, like the officers, during the campaign sworn to loyalty to the Landgrave and to the King of England.

The chaplains accompanied their regiments on the march and in battle. (The Waldeck chaplain, Philipp Waldeck, and the Brunswick chaplain, Melsheimer, were wounded.) [I have found no supporting information to substantiate this statement.]

Insofar as the military operations allowed, the chaplains conducted religious services on a regular basis, when in camp and in winter quarters, every Sunday and prayer hour every Tuesday and Friday.

Whenever possible, a church in the locality was used. Otherwise, they made do as best possible. Religious services were often held in the open air. The liturgy was as practiced in Germany.

Although the differences between the Luthern and Reformed were strongly stressed at that time, the church prayer was the same for everyone.

"We ask you to watch over the rulers of the earth, whom you have sent to rule over us. Take the British King and the entire royal family under your protection. Bless his reign, and give success to his plans and undertakings, bless his forces against his enemies, and crown them with the desired good fortune and blessing. Protect the Prince of our land and the entire Hessian ruling house, and send your blessings from on high. Great Jehovah, from whom the holy power, good council, and righteous strength comes, be with us and do not forsake us. Stand by us and especially safeguard our commanding general, bless his plans and undertakings. Also take into your protection our entire general staff, the staff and other officers, privates, and all those who belong to this regiment."

The needs and circumstances of war have softened these small particulars, or caused them to completely disappear. We know, for instance, of no officially assigned Catholic chaplains. At the start of the war they were not necessary, as the regiments, raised on a regional basis came from only purely Evangelical areas. Only later, during the course of the war, when recruiters were told to expand their efforts into regions with Catholic populations, did Catholics appear among the troops. Even then, they were ministered to by the Evangelical chaplains. (See the church books of Coester and [Henrich] Kuemmell.)

Attendance at religious service was "duty"; attendance at the prayer hour, optional. From information available, however, it seems the prayer hours were well attended.

Six soldiers from each company were allowed to take their families from home with them on the campaign. That explains the large number of baptisms in the records of the chaplains. Marriages performed in violation were not recognized in Germany. Those who did so, were helped by being allowed to remarry after returning to Germany.

After the return to Germany, the chaplains were granted a small pension until they could find a secure position.

The records, which the chaplains maintained during their tour of duty, were considered to be of a private nature by the military units; the personal possession of the chaplains. Therefore, they were never collected at a central location, and most have been lost during the course of time, with few exceptions, when the former chaplains added them to the church records when they took a position as a "civilian pastor".

That is also the explanation as to why cases of soldiers' deaths appear only occasionally in the notices. These "appendices" (and likewise additions from the recruit transports from Germany) were recorded in the regimental orderly rooms, which had to report, in a prescribed format the active and inactive troop strength each month.

How could the American public believe the propaganda put out by the rebels? The Hessian soldiers were accompanied by chaplains, and their Articles of War required regular attendance at religious services. Most diaries kept by the soldiers mention these truths, and religion must have been as important to the men as training to shoot and march.

Chaplains, that I have identified, that accompanied the various units were:

Anhalt Zerbst Regiment - Johann Gottlieb Siegismund Braunsdorf

Ansbach Regiment - Johann Christoph Wagner
Bayreuth Regiment - Georg Christoph Elias Erb
Ansbach-Bayreuth Jaegers - Johann Philipp Erb

Brunswick - Prince Ludwig Dragoon Regiment Carl Melsheimer
Prince Frederick Regiment - Horador, later Schrader
Riedesel Regiment - Melices

Hesse-Hanau - Hesse-Hanau Infantry Regiment- Kaup

HESSIAN CHAPLAINS

Waldeck -Waldeck Regiment - Philipp Waldeck

Hesse-Cassel chaplains, listed by a German writer named Worsinger, were:

Knyphausen and Lossberg Regiments - Wilhelm Bauer (Reformed) from Altmorschen. - Matriculated at Marburg 25 October 1776. Entered captivity on 26 December 1776 after the defeat at Trenton. Exchanged, he went to Canada with these regiments in 1780 and returned to Hesse with the Lossberg Regiment in 1783, From 1786 to 1814 he was the pastor at Moershausen.

Donop Regiment - Friedrich Becker (Reformed) the son of the garrison chaplain Peter Becker in Carlshafen, and his wife, a daughter of the Doctor of Medicine Ebert in Marburg. Went to America with a [recruit] transport for the von Donop Regiment.

Staff Chaplain in 1776 - Karl Becker (Reformed) - brother of Friedrich Becker. Chaplain in the large Hessian hospital on Long Island in 1782. After the war, pastor at Bornich, near St. Goasrshausen. His widow, Sophia Louisa requested the Hesse-Cassel legislature in 1831 to pay credits owed to her husband since the American War. The request was refused.

Staff chaplain in 1776 - Johann Wilhelm Bigel (Reformed) from Cassel. Matriculated at Marburg 18 October 1759. Campaigned from 1776 to 1781. Became deacon at St. Goar in 1781, and on 28 March 1786, Reformed inspector. On 9 March 1801 pastor and inspector at Nastaetten. Died at Nastaetten on 25 October 1815.

Von Donop and von Lossberg Regiments - Georg Christoph Coester son of Pastor Johann Georg Coester in Ersen and Hofgeismar, and Anna Martha, daughter of Pastor Mathias Waere in Bruena. He was baptized 15 December 1751 in Ersen and matriculated at Marburg on 17 April 1771. In 1776 assigned to the von Donop Garrison Regiment at Homberg/Efza. 1 August 1786 to 14 July 1790 pastor in Malsfeld. Died 14 July 1790 in Malsfeld. Married his cousin, Dorothea Coester. Children 1) Georg Christoph Bernhard, born 30 March 1788 in Malsfeld. Treasurer in Homberg and Neustadt; died Oberrlistungen. Godfather - Johann Christian Coester, Ersen 2) Henrich Wilhelm, born 6 July 1780 in Malsfeld, Died 6 March 1862 in Homberg. 1833-1853 pastor in Obervorshuete. Godfather - Henrich Justus Coester, deacon in Vacha (brother of his father).

Mirbach Regiment - Johann Christoph Eskucke (Lutheran) - son of pastor and professor Balthsar

Ludwig Eskucke in Rinteln, and his wife Catharina Florentine, nee Faucher. Born 1751 in Rinteln. Studied in Rinteln, Goettingen, and after 11 May 1773, in Marburg. Died 10 May 1776 at Bremerlehe, prior to embarkation.

Wissenbach Garrison Regiment - Johann Conrad Grimmel (Reformed) - son of the merchant, Martin Grimmel of Cassel, and his wife, Anna Catherina Elizabeth, nee Eskucke. Born at Cassel on 8 September 1753. Matriculated 2 July 1774. 1776 with the Wissenbach Garrison Regiment. Married Anna Juliane Grimmel at Ziegenhain 26 December 1784. Died 26 June 1789 (34 years old.).

Hereditary Prince Regiment - Johann Georg Hausknecht (Reformed) - Son of Johann Wilhelm Hausknecht, who was in Hessian service. Born 18 October 1750. Matriculated at 11 April 1768. 1776 with the Hereditary Prince Regiment. Taken into captivity with the Regiment on 19 October 1781 at Yorktown. Released on parole to New York. 1784 pastor and court chaplain in Philippstal. 1785 pastor in Bockenheim, where the German Reformed District of Frankfurt am Main was headquartered. 1786 pastor in the District of Frankfurt am Main. Consistorial Councilor. Died 2 December 1812. Married Christine Maria Anna Krafft, from Cassel, at Frankfurt am Main on 15 June 1790. (She was born in 1760, daughter of the pastor Justus Christoph Krafft, and died at Hanau on 30 September 1850.)

Staff Chaplain - Supposedly Georg Friedrich Heller, son of Johann Georg Heller in Fambach near Schmalkalden, and Martha Elisabeth, nee Loeber.

Von Huyne and von Buenau Regiments - Henrich Kuemmell (Reformed) - son of Adam Friedrich Kuemmell, second pastor at Vacha, and Christine Charlotta, nee Bodenstein. Born 6 December 1753. Matriculated at Rinteln in 1771 and at Marburg on 29 April 1774. 1776-1783 chaplain with the von Huyne and von Buenau Regiments. 1784 second pastor of the Reformed Schmalkalden District, 1803 inspector of the Reformed District. Also castle and first pastor of the Reformed District. He died 17 December 1830. On 15 February 1785 he married Catharina Margaretha Reimann at Herrenbreitungen. (She was born 8 February 1764 at Heerenbreitungen and died 22 July 1827 at Schmalkalden. She was the daughter of Reformed pastor Georg Philipp Reimann at Herrenbreitungen.)

Field hospital chaplain - Johann Konrad Henrich Schrecker - Son of Pastor Henrich Schrecker in Schmalkalden. Confirmed Easter 1761. 1771-1776 assistant in Heineback. Since January 1776, chaplain.

Died Altmorschen 30 June 1785. (47 years, 11 months old) previous chaplain with the Hessian Corps in America.

Georg Christiann Stern, son of the first Forest Secretary in Marburg. Matriculated at Marburg 22 March 1754 and 31 March 1768. 1776 chaplain. Deacon in Melsungen. 1789 pastor in Nordhausen. Died 28 November 1793 by jumping into the Fulda River due to melancholy. On 15 September 1784 married Wilhelmina Juliana Wiesler, who died in November 1798, 31 and ½ years old, daughter of the court gardener, Johannes Wiesler in the Karl's Garden (Karlsaue) at Cassel.

Rall and Young Lossberg Regiments - Rudolf Reinhard Virnau, born 4 January 1749 in Wellershausen, son of the teacher at that place, Johannes Virnau, and Anna Margaretha, nee Beyer, living in Wellershausen. (After 1751, her parents lived in Netra.) Matriculated at Marburg 16 April 1768, 1771 rector at Felsberg. 1776 chaplain with the Rall and Young Lossberg Regiments. Campaigned 1776-1783. April 1784 pastor in Sachsenhausen, District of Ziegenhain. Died there of a high fever 21 May 1785. Married Wilhelmina Peffer of Marburg.

Leib Regiment - Johann Christoph Weidemann, born at Cassel Court District 19 September 1751, son of the court clerk, Johann Wilhelm Weidemann, and Anna Catherina, nee Hundeshagen. Matriculated at Marburg 26 June 1770. 1779 chaplain with the Leib Regiment. Campaign 1779-1783. Died at New York. His younger brother was missing as a free corporal in the same regiment, on a transport ship on the crossing (to America).

[The above information was translated from Gesichtliche Nachrichten aus Treysa (Historical Reports from Treysa), 1969, as is the introduction and the diary and church book of G. C. Coester which follow.]

In the pages which follow, when the German writer used an *in* ending on the family names of females, I have also retained this spelling of the names.

Church Book
of
Hesse-Cassel Chaplain
Georg C. Coester

HESSIAN CHAPLAINS

PROTOCOL

The ministry acts of Chaplain G.C. Coester performed with the illustrious von Donop and von Lossberg Regiments (and others).

Begun on 14 March 1776

In the possession of the Parsonage, Malsfeld, Hesse

Inventar II S, 68/69 A. c. Nr. 28

Born and Baptized of the Illustrious von Donop Regiment during the Time I [Georg C. Coester] Served It as Chaplain

- - - - - - - -

Hamilton Carl Henrich Haemer - Johannes Haemer's, musketeer in Lieutenant Colonel Company, legitimate son, was born to Martha Elisabeth Haemer, nee Lohr, on 25 March 1776, at three o'clock in the morning on our trip to America, on the Atlantic Ocean, aboard the English transport ship *Jenny*. The ship's captain, William Hamilton, Lieutenant Colonel [Karl Philipp] Heymel, and Lieutenant [Johann Henrich] von Bardeleben were asked to be sponsors. The ship's captain was the first, but because he was a Scotsman and a Presbyterian, he did not wish to hold the child to be baptized. His excuse was that it was not customary in his country, and second, as he was always at sea, he could not fill the duty which a sponsor has. This excuse seemed valid to me. Lieutenant Colonel Heymel therefore held the child to be baptized, and gave the child the name Hamilton Karl Henrich. The name Hamilton it received from the ship's captain, over his objection, because he said if he should get to Hesse, or if the child came to England, I will recognize his name, and then I will take care of him. This festive occasion was conducted while the sea was rather calm, on the following day, the 24th of March. He was the first child that I baptized and possibly the first Hessian to be baptized aboard a transport ship on the Atlantic Ocean. [NB] -The child and his mother died in the autumn of 1777.

Robert Scheffer - born to Johann Henrich Scheffer, corporal in Major Hinte's Company, and Elisabeth Scheffer, during the night of 11 - 12 July 1776, on our voyage to America, on the English transport ship *Hope*. Because we had good weather and calm seas on 16 July, I was taken across in a small boat. I baptized him. Robert Peacock, captain of the ship *Hope*, held it to be baptized.

Arietha Martha Elisabeth - born to Christoph Abel, musketeer in the von Donop Regiment, and his wife Catharina, nee Martin, a daughter, on 12 July 1776, during our voyage from Halifax to New York, on the English transport ship *Empress*, and was baptized in my presence by Chaplain Hausknecht of the Herditary Prince Regiment. The sponsor was Martha Elisabeth, wife of Quartermaster Sergeant Henrich Philipp Roemer of that regiment. The baptism took place on 2 August 1776.

Catherina Elisabeth - a daughter, was born to

Johannes Scheffer, musketeer of Colonel von Gose's Company, of the von Donop Regiment, and his wife, Anna Elisabeth, nee Herd, from Roemersfeld, District of Borken, on 9 October 1776 on New York Island [Manhattan], in the camp at Blumenthal, at three o'clock in the morning, and baptized the following day, 10 October. The sponsor was Catherina Elisabeth, wife of Corporal Johann Hassanpflug of Colonel von Gose's Company. [NB\ Died at New York 19 September 1783.

Catherina Elisabeth - illegitimate daughter of Musketeer Adam Sustmann, of Colonel von Gose's Company, born at Wabern, and Maria Elisabeth Wiederhold, born at Gutenborn, District of Borken, on 6 November 1776, at seven o'clock in the evening, in the camp on New York Island, and baptized on the ninth of that month. The sponsor Catherina Elisabeth, wife of Corporal Johann Hassenpflug of Colonel von Gose's Company. The woman, left behind, I do not know why, by her intended husband, who had promised marriage, had followed. She arrived with our second fleet, sought out her husband-to-be, and, as she set her first foot in his tent, gave birth to a young daughter. [NB -Died at Philadelphia.]

Johann Adam - son of Joachim Kurz, musketeer in Captain von Kutzleben's Company, and his wife,

Anna Catherina, nee Viemann, of Zimmersrode, District of Borken, was born between eight and nine o'clock in the evening of 16 December in our winter quarters in the city of New York. I baptized him on 19 December. The sponsor was Adam Schmeck, drummer of the regiment.

Johannes - son of Adam Schmeck, drummer of Colonel von Gose's Company, and his wife, Anna Martha, was born on the night of 30 December 1776, in our winter quarters at New York, and baptized on 2 January 1777. The sponsor was Johannes Lumpe, who had been the servant of Captain [Friedrich Karl] von Weitershausen.

HESSIAN CHAPLAINS

**NB - On 9 January 1777, I was
Transferred to the von Donop
Brigade by His Excellence,
Lieutenant General [Leopold] von Heister.
The first child I Baptized was:**

- - - - - - - -

Johann Georg - son of Grenadier Abel Trumpf, of Wolfsanger, District of Cassel, and his wife, Anna Catherina, of Sondershausen, District of Cassel, who was born at four o'clock in the afternoon of 24 January 1777, at New Brunswick, in New Jersey, in America. I baptized him on 26 January 1777. Sponsor was Johann Georg Schwarz, a grenadier in the Leib Regiment, born in Weninzenhausen.

Anna Catherina - legitimate daughter of Johann Henrich Otto, grenadier in Lieutenant Colonel von Minnegerode's Battalion, and his wife, Angelica Dorothea Stark, born at Grebenstein, was born at four o'clock in the morning, on 29 January 1777, at New Brunswick in the province of New Jersey, and baptized there on 31 January 1777. Sponsor Anna Catherina, wife of Johann Krueck, grenadier in the same battalion.

Catherina Elisabeth - legitimate daughter of Grenadier Johannes Schmidt, of the Koehler Grenadier Battalion, and Dorothea Elisabeth, nee Erb, of Friedewald, was born on 18 February 1777, between eleven and twelve o'clock noon, at the winter quarters at New Brunswick, in the province of New Jersey, and baptized on 20 February 1777. Sponsor was Catherina Elisabeth, wife of Grenadier Johann Iffert, of the Koehler Battalion.

David - son of Johann Reinhard Hemce, grenadier of the von Linsing Grenadier Battalion, and his wife, Margaretha, nee Eismann, of Hanau, was born on 19 February 1777 at Brunswick, during the morning of, and baptized 21 February 1777. Sponsor David Frise, grenadier of the von Linsing Battalion.

Maria Magdalena - legitimate daughter of Johann Paulus Schuck, sergeant in the Koehler, and his wife, Anna Christina Becker of Zierenberg, was born on 20 February 1777 at New Brunswick, and baptized 23 February. Sponsor was Maria Magdalena, wife of Sergeant Netze, of the Guard Battalion.

Wilhelm Philipp - legitimate son of Grenadier Adam Koch, Sr., of the Vacant Grenadier Company of the von Donop Regiment, from Oberbeisheim, District of Homberg, and his wife, Maria Dorothea, of Hergetsfeld, District of Homberg, was born about four o'clock in the afternoon of 8 March 1777 at New Brunswick, and baptized the following day. Sponsor was [Philipp Wilhelm] von Gall, present commander of the Vacant Grenadier Company.

Dorothea Elisabeth - daughter of Grenadier Peter Stange, of the von Lengercke , and his wife, Catherina Elisabeth, first saw the light of day during our sea voyage from New York to Philadelphia, on 29 June 1777, and was baptized by me on 27 August. Sponsor was Dorothea Elisabeth, wife of Grenadier Johannes Gromann.

Johann George - legitimate son of Joseph Carl Wielteck, hunting horn player of the Ansbach Field Jaeger Company, And his wife, Fredrica Heinerica, was born on 13 November 1777, at Philadelphia, between eight and nine o'clock in the morning, and baptized by me on the following day, 14 November 1777.Sponsor was Johann Georg Bauer, field jaeger of Captain von Ewald's Company.

Johann George - legitimate son of Conrad Hase, grenadier of Captain von Gall's Company, of the von Donop Regiment, and his wife, Anna Elisabeth, was born on 27 November 1777, at Philadelphia, and baptized in this city on 29 November. Sponsor was Johann Georg Hase, of the 2nd Guard Battalion.

NB - Anna Elisabeth - legitimate daughter of Jacob Hartmann, musketeer of the Leib Company of the von Donop Regiment, and his wife, Christina, nee Landau, of Lelbach, District of Hayna, saw the light of day in the camp at Philadelphia, on 29 November 1777, and was baptized on 30 November. [Sponsor] was Anna Elisabeth, wife of Philipp Guembell, musketeer in the von Kutzleben Company of the von Donop Regiment.

Henrich Wilhelm - legitimate son of Christoph Humburg, field jaeger in the 1st Hessian Field Jaeger Company, and his wife, Elisabeth Blum, born at Gudensberg, first saw the light of day in the camp at Philadelphia on 27 November 1777. I baptized him on the first day of Christmas month [December] 1777. His sponsor was Johann Henrich Gottfried Huene, field jaeger of the 1st Hessian Field Jaeger Company.

Johann Friedrich - legitimate son of Peter Paul Wirth, jaeger of the Hessian Field Jaeger Corps, and his wife, Gertruth, born at Nastaetten, District of Reinfels, was born to the world, at Philadelphia, on 30 December 1777, at three o'clock in the afternoon. I baptized him on 5 January 1778. Sponsors were Johann Ewald, captain of the Jaeger Company, and Friedrich Adam Julius von Wangenheim, Hessian officer of the Jaeger Corps.

HESSIAN CHAPLAINS

On 1 January 1778, I was again Relieved by Staff Chaplain Heller On the Order of His Excellence, Lieutenant General von Heister. And Returned to the von Donop Regiment

----

Maria Magdalena -an illegitimate child, whose mother was Maria Magdalena Obersteig. Sponsor Susanna Aug, wife of a Philadelphia resident She said Christian Krause, musketeer of the von Knyphausen Regiment, was the father. NB - This person later married an Englishman.

Martha Elisabeth - the legitimate daughter of Recruit Nicolaus Barthel, born at Gernrode on the Eichsfelde, and his wife, Anna Catherina Schwarzbach, from Erfurth, (wedding certificate of Pastor Vilmar, 20 June 1777, at Cassel), was born on an English ship, on the voyage to America, on 21 March 1776, and baptized by me at Philadelphia on 10 May. Sponsor was Martha Elisabeth, wife of Corporal Reinhardt Roemer, of the Leib Company, of the von Donop Regiment.

Johann Adam - was born on 22 November 1778, and baptized on 23 November 1778. Sponsor was Johann Adam Schmeck, of Colonel von Gose's

Company. The father was Johann Kurz, of Major von Kutzleben's Company, and the mother's name was Anna Catherina, nee Viemann, of Zimmersrode, District of Borken. This poor child was a complete abortion, and had a growth like a turtle on his head. After conferring with Regimental Surgeon [Johann Jacob] Stieglitz, who considered it a human being, it was baptized in God's name. It died a quarter hour later. I was glad!

Baptized in the Leib Regiment
(Pastor Weidemann sick)

Maria Catherina - born on 8 October 1778; baptized on 15 October 1778. The father was Jost Henrich Weising, of the Leib Company. Gertrud Helmich, from Simmershausen, District of Cassel. Sponsor was Maria Catherina, wife of Sergeant [Samuel] Blum of Captain Waltenberg's Company..

Baptized in the von Truembach Regiment

Berthold - born on 25 October 1778; baptized on 1 January 1779. Father - Christian Schelm, musketeer in Colonel von Muenchhausen's Company; mother - Elisabeth Bolt, from Hofgeismar; sponsor - Berthold Koch, of Captain Scheer's Company.

HESSIAN CHAPLAINS

List of those Persons whom I married during theTime I Served As Chaplain of the von Donop Regiment

In Hesse

1) Adan Schuchard, - sergeant in Lieutenant Colonel Heymel's Company, with Anna Martha Jacob, from Homberg. Homberg, 14 February 1776. NB - This Adam Schuchard cut his throat in the hospital at New York in 1782.

2) Reinhart Ludwig - musketeer in Major Hinte's Company, Gertruth Sophie Zelazin, from [blank], Homberg, 14 February 1776.

3) Adam Scheck - drummer in Colonel von Gose's Company, with Anna Martha Volhars, from Allendorf,, on der Ohm, Schweinsberg District. Homberg, 14 February 1776.

4) Wilhelm Schroeder - musketeer in the Colonel's Company, with Anna Catherina Ritberg, from Jesberg. Homberg, 14 February 1776.

5) Philipp Guembell - musketeer in Captain von Kutzleben's Company, with Anna Elisabeth Pflueger, from Homberg. Homberg, 14 February 1776.

6) Paul Trischmann - musketeer in the Leib

Company, with Catharina Schneider, from Remsfeld, on 14 February 1776.

7) Georg Schroeder - musketeer in Captain von Kutzleben's Company, with Anna Catherina Braun, from Gumbeth. Homberg, 14 February 1776.

8) Johannes Hessler - musketeer in the Leib Company, with Anna Catherina Riel, from Gumbeth on 21 February 1776.

9) Johannes Ide - musketeer in Lieutenant Colonel Heymel's Company, with Anna Elisabeth Weber, from Waldesbruech. Homberg, 28 February 1776.

10) Henrich Wolff - musketeer in Major Hinte's Company with [blank]. Homberg, 28 February 1776.

11) Johannes Wahl - musketeer in Lieutenant Colonel Heymel's Company, with Anna Martha Scheuer, from Reptich, District of Borken. Homberg, 29 February 1776.

12) Johannes Scheffer - musketeer in Colonel von Gose's Company, with Anna Elisabeth Hars, from Roemersberg. Homberg, 28 February 1776.

13) Henrich Kehl - corporal in the Leib Company, Maria Sabina Fuchs, daughter of Pastor Fuchs of Remsfeld. Homburg, 29 February 1776.

14) Conrad Riehl - musketeer in Colonel Heymel's Company, wife Anna Martha Schanz, from

Odenborn. Homberg, 29 February 1776.

15) Henrich Wernert - grenadier in Captain von Weitershausen's Company, with Anna Martha Rimmel, from Verna, on the march to Heiligenrode, 2 March 1776.

16) Joachim Kurz - musketeer in Captain von Kutzleben's Company, with Anna Catherina Viemann, from Zimmersrode, District of Borken, on the march to Uschlag, in Hannover, 17 March 1776.

17) Johannes Haemer, musketeer in the Lieutenant Colonel's Company, with Maria Elisabeth Lohr, from Freudenthal, on the march to Ronnebeck, District of Blumenthal, in Hannover, 17 March 1776.

18) Johannes Sustmann - musketeer in Colonel von Gose's Company, with Maria Elisabeth Wiederhold, daughter of the deceased resident, Reinhard Wiederhold, born in Udenborn, District of Borken. Married in America, on New York Island, in the camp at Blumenthal on 20 November 1776. (NB - Due to insufficient funds, the groom could not pay the usual eight Reichsthalers. Colonel [David Ephraim] von Gose promised that it would be paid later.)

19) Leonora Luisa - the small daughter of Werner Dickhaut, musketeer in the von Donop Regiment, and Anna Catharina Pickhard, both born at Holzhausen, District of Homberg, was born at New

York on 10 April 1777, and baptized on the thirteenth, because I was present there. The sponsor was Leonora Luisa, wife of Corporal Toerfels, of the Leib Company,

At this point is Jacob, runner for Colonel von Donop. He married a girl from Brunswick, in America, with the consent of his chief, at Kreton, in the spring of 1777. The wife died at Brunswick, on Long Island, in December 1779. (NB - This woman died at Brunswick, in the fall of 1779.)

On 31 August, I married Johann Letzerich, non-commissioned officer of Captain Wach's 1st Company of the Hereditary Prince Regiment, and Martha Wacker, former wife of the killed-in-action Corporal Wacker, in the camp at Head of Elk.

On 15 September 1777, I married the Hessian jaeger Conrad Sackert, of Major Prueschenck's Company, and Carolina Wetzler, Sebbeterode. This took place in the camp not far from Dellweth, in Pennsylvania. NB - Major Prueschenck promised to collect the consent money, and give it to me. NB - Six days later the woman was chased out of camp for being a prostitute.

On 2 December 1777, I married Johann Burschel, grenadier from Captain Blesen's Company, of the Guard Battalion, and Sophia Meien, born at

Cassel, and widow of [the soldier] Meien, at Philadelphia, NB - [No entry.]

On 19 December 1777, at Philadelphia, I married Grenadier Abraham Loehler of the von Lengercke Grenadier Battalion, and the young girl, Elisabeth Well, from Hesse-Hanau. The first marriage which I performed as a result of my duty with the von Lossberg Regiment, in the winter huts at Marsten's Wharf, 1776-1779.

After requesting permission of Colonel von Loos, and the approval of Auditor Heymel, I married the following persons in the winter huts at Hellgate, on 17 January 1779:

Fusilier Friedrich Busch, of the von Lossberg Regiment, born in Schermbach, in Bueckeburg, 24 years old, and Wilhelmina Catherina, nee Ohm, widow of the dead fusilier Ludwig Clausing, of the mentioned von Lossberg Regiment. The groom was a foreigner, and therefore did not have to pay the eight Thaler fee. NB - The bride lost her husband only 21 weeks previously, therefore I could not marry her because of possible pregnancy, as cited in the law covering a year's mourning, but Captain (Major Ludwig August von) Hanstein and several other officers convinced me that the mentioned Wilhelmina Catherina - following the death of her previous husband - two weeks thereafter - had given birth, so because of the unavoidable circumstance of the war, I made no objection to the marriage.

Flushing on Long Island, 1 January 1781

After Carl Ludolph, grenadier of the von Lossberg Fusilier Regiment, born at Oldenburg, District of Schaumburg, received permission of his commander, Lieutenant Colonel [Wilhelm] von Loewenstein, to marry the widow, Rosina Charlotta Leytmeier, also born in Oldenburg, and after paying the eight Reichsthalers, and swearing an oath about his single status, the mentioned grenadier, after complying with the above requirements, was married on the above date to his bride without further objections. NB - The widow, whose former husband had been killed during the siege of Charleston in April 1780, had not yet completed her year of mourning, but because his wife had not accompanied him [to South Carolina], there was no possibility of her being pregnant from her former husband.

New York, 13 January 1783, von Donop Regiment Marriage

After Henrich Merten, soldier serving in Major von Kutzleben's Company, of the von Donop Regiment, born at Zwesten, District of Borken, received permission to marry, paid the eight

Reichsthalers, in cash, for the maintenance of the Carlshaven Hospital, for his first marriage, been approved by the auditor, and also been warned about swearing a false oath, and sworn that he was single, I married him to his betrothed bride, Anna Gertruth Villgraff, nee Schick, born in Abterode, District of Witzenhausen, widow of the dead Grenadier Erhard Villgraff, of the von Linsing Grenadier Battalion, after being shown the death certificate. NB - I gave each of them a marriage certificate at New York, on 14 January 1783, as proof of the marriage.

Marriage

Upon having received permission, as well as having taken an oath that he was single, and because there was no other objection, the soldier Michael Bernhard, of the Leib Company, of the von Donop Regiment, a foreigner born at Schwicks, in Lothringen, was married by a priest to his betrothed bride, Charlotte de la Lime, daughter of Mr. Jean Baptiste La Lime, a resident of Quebec. NB - Both were Catholic.

Marriage

On 20 July 1783, I married upon presentation of permission to marry from His Excellency, Lieutenant General [Friedrich Wilhelm] von Lossberg, Casimir Theodor Goerke, lieutenant of artillery, with the young lady, Elisabeth Roosewel, born at New York.

Deaths

On 19 September 1781, at nine o'clock in the morning, Gemeling, the 66 year old sutler of the von Donop Regiment. I found by this man a firm belief, and his trust in God's grace, was unfailing to the end. Fort Knyphausen.

On 5 February 1782, Conrad Giese, from Hundshausen, in the Judicial District of Jesberg, died. During his final years, he was the cook for Colonel von Heymel, the commander of the von Donop Regiment. I was not told his age. His end was the easy death of a Christian, who trusted his Redeemer to take him to a better world. He took communion twelve hours before his death.

Penance Situations in the von Donop Regiment

On 14 March 1776, I dismissed (the penance payment) of the following musketeers and their brides, namely, Georg Schroeder, of Kutzleben's Company, and his wife, Anna Catherina Braun, and secondly, the Musketeer Johannes Hessler, of the Leib Company, and his wife, Marie Catherina Riel, from Gumbeth.

Johann Adam Sustmann, and his bride, Maria Elisabeth Wiederhold, stated their repentance to me on 20 November 1776, at New York, when I married them in America.

Johann Henrich Kramer, from Gilsa, District of Borken, was forgiven his penance payment on 24 December 1776, at New York, because of a situation with Anna Elisabeth Truemper, of Reptig, District of Borken.

Penance Situations with the Donop Brigade
At New Brunwick on 1 March 1777

1) From the Koehler Grenadier Battalion

    A. From Captain Bode's Company

        Grenadier Johann Holzapfel - (I gave the certificate on 6 September 1783.)

        Grenadier Conrad Killen - (I gave the certificate on 30 August 1783.)

        Grenadier Koch - (I gave the certificate on 6 September 1783.)

Grenadier [Georg] Borck - (I gave the certificate on 30 August 1783.)
 B. Captain Hohenstein's Company
  Grenadier Georg Weber
  Grenadier Johann Jost Habber
  Grenadier Henrich Roese - (I gave the certificate on 1 November 1783.)

New Brunswick, 17 March 1783
From the von Minnegerode Grenadier Battalion

 A. The non-commissioned officer Johann Georg Fehr, of the Vacant Company of the Hereditary Prince Regiment, born at Grebenau, District of Milsungen.
  B. From Captain von Stein's Grenadier Company
 Grenadier Christian Well, born at Treysa
 Grenadier Conrad Spohr, Lingelbach, Judicial District of Doernberg

At Easter, 30 March 1777
From the Minnigerode Grenadier Battalion

 Grenadier Justus Decker, of Captain von Stein's Company, from Arenborn, District of Feckerhagen
 Grenadier Bernhard Schroeder, of Captain von Stein's Company, from [Gross] Ropperhausen, District

of Ziegenhain

Grenadier Henrich Weber, Sr., from Stein, near Hattendorf, District of Neukirchen

Grenadier Christoph Thomas, of the Vacant Company, of the Hereditary Prince Regiment, from Neuerode, the Judicial District of Poeneburg

At Philadelphia, on 28 February 1778, Musketeer Johannes Schneider, of Colonel Hinte's Company of the von Donop Regiment, born at Felsberg, came to me and said he had committed an act of fornication with Elisabeth Assemann, from Felsberg. He was sorry for having committed the sin, and promised to marry the unfortunate girl upon his return. As he then took communion, I dismissed payment of the penance.

Jamaica, on Long Island

On 23 December 1780, Grenadier Christoph Blum, of Von Gall's Company, of the von Lengercle Battalion, from Roemersberg, came to me and said that he had committed an act of fornication with Anna Catherina Wenderoth, born at Malsfeld, and the child, which was a girl, was still living. He promised to marry the woman.

Jamaica, on Long Island

On 30 October 1780, Artillery Sergeant Johann Henrich Brethauer, of the Leib Company, born at

Klein Almerode, came to me and said that he had made an American girl, Polly Tiezen, from New York, pregnant, and his child was still living. If he could be given permission, he would marry the woman, but in any case, would always support the child and its mother.

At Jamaica, on 30 October 1780

Johann Pflueger, of Captain von Gall's Company, of the von Donop Regiment, from Wallenstein, District of Homberg, came to me and said he had committed an act of fornication with Catherina Elisabeth Aulbel, from Falkenberg. According to later reports, the child was a son, born on Whitsuntide 1777, and died four weeks later. NB - He promised to marry the woman.

At Flushing, on 30 December 1780

Grenadier Burghard Zehr, of the von Knyphausen Regiment, born at Roelshausen, District of Neukirchen, declared that he had made a girl from New York pregnant, that he was truly sorry for his sin, and that to clear his conscience, would like to have communion. As he swore on his oath to be more careful in the future, and especially promised to conduct himself as a proper soldier, I allowed him to take communion with a clear conscience. [Pages 27 through 31, of the manuscript, are blank.)

PS

Conrad Frey - the eldest son of Georg Adolf Frey, of Grossenkeder, and his wife, Anna Margaretha, from Vacha, was born on 17 June 1778, on the English transport ship *Charming Nancy*, during the voyage from Philadelphia to New York, and baptized in the camp at Marsten's Wharf, on Manhattan Island. Conrad Numme, of Donnershausen, groom for Major General von Gose (the colonel and commander of the von Donop Regiment), was the sponsor. I issued a baptismal certificate on 3 October 1783.

Register of Children Baptized in 1782

Anna Catherina - daughter of Georg Haynlain, musketeer in the von Kutzleben Company, of the von Donop Regiment, born in the Principality of Elbangen, and the city of the same name, and his wife, Maria Catherina, nee Friederick, born at Carlaun, in Zweibruecken, was legitimately born at Murray's house, not far from New York, at eight o'clock in the morning, on 24 February 1782, and baptized on the 27th of the same month and year, by me. The sponsor was Anna Catherina, nee Viemann, of Zimmersrode, wife of a musketeer of Major von Kutzleben's Company, of the same regiment, by the name of Joachim Kurz. (The baptism certificate was sent to Nova Scotia on 6 September 1783.)

HESSIAN CHAPLAINS

Prince Charles Regiment

Catharina Elisabeth - was born on the morning of 17 April 1782, on Manhattan Island, about six miles from New York City, and as her chaplain was not available, she was baptized by me on 19 April 1782, Johann Dietrich Pauly, born at Sontra, of the 4th [Company], and gunsmith of the Prince Charles Regiment, was the father. The mother was Elisabeth Haselbach, born at Rauschenberg. Catharina Elisabeth Sandmoeller, wife of the soldier [Friedrich] Sandmoeller, of the Leib Company, of the Prince Charles Regiment, born at Gilsa, District of Borken, was the sponsor.

Von Donop Regiment

Johann Valentin Engelhard - legitimate child, was born on 21 June 1782, in the camp near Fort Knyphausen, and baptized on the 23rd of the same month and year. The father was Christian Engelhard, soldier in the Leib Company, of the von Donop Regiment, and the mother was Eva Barbara Kahlstuetzer. Both parents were born in the same village, that is, Oberbergen, near Schmalkalden. A non-commissioned officer of the Young von Lossberg Regiment, by the name of Johann Valentin Herdmann, of the Leib Company, was the sponsor.

Miss Sarah Patterson, a lawful daughter of Mr. Stephan Patterson, assistant in the General Commissary. Mrs. Sarah Patterson, was born on the 5th day of June 1782, and christened by my ministry on 28 June 1782. Mr. Tuck, lieutenant of the British Legion, and Mrs. Falkener, both performed the duty of goships The place where Miss Sarah Patterson is born and baptized is called Harlem Valley, 10 miles north of New York. I gave the certificate on 22 September 1782. *Mortua est.* [This sentence is in English in the original. Gossip, not goship, is a no-longer used form meaning godparent. *Mortua est* is lined out in the original.]

Von Donop Regiment
Baptism certificate issued 15 May 1785

Bernhard Vogt - a legitimate son, was born during the night of 9 to 10 July 1782, in the camp near Fort Knyphausen, and baptized by me on the 12th day of the same month and year. Jacob Vogt, a Catholic, born at Fritzlar and presently a soldier in the Leib Company of the von Donop Regiment, was the father, and Christina Sophia, born at Hannover Minden, was the mother. Bernhard Naumann, soldier of the same company, and born at Allmuthshausen, District of Homberg, in Hesse, was their baptismal witness. NB - Jacob Vogt, a very bad individual, much given to gambling and drinking, deserted from our service at New York in the year 1783.

Von Donop Regiment

Kilian Gassert - legitimate son, was born at New York on 29 January 1783, and baptized on 2 February 1783. Joseph Gassert, a soldier in Colonel Heymel's Company, of the von Donop Regiment, born at Wuerzburg, and of the Catholic religion, was the father, and his wife, Eva Catharina, nee Linninger, from Aptey Everach, the mother. Kilian Klee, a soldier of the same company, from Zentersbach, in the Schwarzenfels [Zuentersbach, below Schluec-ternd] was the sponsor.

Von Donop Regiment

Catharina Elisabeth -a legitimate daughter of the Musketeer Conrad Hirsch, of Major von Kutzleben's Company, of the von Donop Regiment, born in Odenheim, in the Pfalz, and his wife, Anna Margaretha, born at Stockstadt, in Darmstadt, saw the light of day at New York on 23 February 1783, and was baptized by me on the 28th of the same month and year. In the name of his wife, Catharina Elisabeth Ditmar, left behind in Hesse, Corporal Johann Wilhelm Ditmar, of the same company, born in Hesse-Homberg, was the sponsor.

Prince Charles Regiment

Elisabeth - legitimate daughter of the corporal by the name of Johannes Zertz, of Major General von Gose's Company, of the Prince Charles Regiment, and his wife nee Pflueger, born at Wickenrode, District of Kaufungen, was born in the Lisboner Brewery, on the North River at New York, was born on 3 March 1783, and baptized by me on the 5th of the same month and year. The godmother was the wife of Jost Eichlers, musketeer in Colonel von Lengercke's Company of the same regiment, Elisabeth Eichlers, born at Kreuzberg, District of Vacha (Philippsthal])

Artillery

Dorothea Elisabeth - legitimate daughter of a cannoneer by the name of Wilhelm Scheffer, born at Cassel, and his wife, Wilhelmina, nee Hanck, from Korback, was born on 25 April 1783 at New York, and baptized on the first of May of the same year. Dorothea Elisabeth Eberhard, wife of Cannoneer Eberhard of the same company, was the godmother. (The mother was also a sponsor.)

von Donop Regiment

Anna Catharina - legitimate daughter of the soldier (of Major von Kutzleben's Company, of the von Donop Regiment), Joachim Kurz, and his wife, Anna Catharina, nee Viemann, from Zimmerstode, was born at New York, on 25 June 1783, at about 2 o'clock in the morning, and baptized on the 29th of the same month and year. Anna Catharina , wife of the soldier Georg Schroeder (Major von Wurmb's Company of the von Donop Regiment,) gave the child its Christian name.

Artillery Regiment

Johannes Katz - the legitimate son of Artillery Sergeant Johannes Caspar Katzmann, of Captain Schleestein's Company, born at Braunenshausen, District of Rothenburg, and his wife, Eva, nee Mayer, from Cassel, was born between nine and ten o'clock, 23 July 1783, at New York, and baptized by me on the 29th of the same month and year. The sponsor was a soldier of Captain Goebel's Company of the von Buenau Regiment, by the name of Johannes Vogeler, born at Sontra. Dd 2 Doll. [This seems to indicate a fee of 2 dollars was paid.]

Young von Lossberg Regiment

Anton Post - was born at New York on 9 August 1783, at ten o'clock in the evening, and baptized by me on the 13th of the same month. Georg Post, from Breidenbach am Herzberge, Judicial District of Duerenberg [Duernberg/Hausen-Herzberg], currently a soldier in the Leib Company, of the Young von Lossberg Regiment, was the father, and his wife,

Anna Kunigunde, of Heckelsmankirchen, by Fulda, the mother. Anton Guise, musketeer of Major Baurmeister's Company, of the same regiment, was the sponsor.

Young von Lossberg Regiment

Eva Catharina Sophia - was born to wedded parents at New York, on 18 August 1783, and baptized on the 24th of the same month. Johann Friedrich Hartwig,, born at Ersrode, District of Ludwigseck, Judicial District of Riedesel, sergeant major of the Leib Company, of the Young von Lossberg Regiment, was the father, and his wife, Anna Catharina, born in New York, daughter of Johann Werner, was the mother. Johann Henrich Reichhard, a non-commissioned officer of the Prince Charles Regiment, held the child in the name of his sister, Eva Catharina Sophia Schultheiss, from Willingshausen, County Hersfeld, District of Niederaula, to be baptized .**NB** - This Hartwig deserted shortly before our embarkation in America.

Artillery

Henrietta Goerke - the legitimate daughter of the Hessian Field Artillery Lieutenant Casimir Theodor Goerke, and his lawful wife, Mrs. Elisabeth Goerke, born at New York, was born near Fort Knyphausen, according to the father's statement, on

16 September 1783 , and baptized at the same place by me on 16 October 1783. Mrs. Margaretha Cozine, wife of Mr. Cozine, a lawyer at New York, and the gentleman, Lieutenant Colonel Hans Heinrich Eitel, commander of the Hessian Artillery in North America, were the solicited sponsors. NB - Seven weeks and four days [later, she died.]

Von Donop Regiment

Anna Catharina - the legitimate daughter of Drummer Adam Schmeck, of Colonel Heymel's Company, and his wife, Anna Martha, was born at New York, on 15 October 1784, and baptized on the 19th of the same month. Sponsor: Reitze Amthauer, soldier of the same company, held the child for baptism in the name of his sister Anna Catharina, from Waltersbrueck. Died on the 21st of the same month, [and in Latin] may the ground rest lightly over her.

Martha Catharina - legitimate daughter, was born in England, at the Royal Barracks, at Chatham, on 21 January 1784, to a grenadier of the von Dithfurth Regiment, by the name of Jacob Dietrich, born at Viermuenden, and his wife, Maria Margaretha, from Altenlotheim, in Darmstadt, and baptized by me on the 25th of the same month and year, with Martha

Catharina, [wife] of a corporal of the Prince Friedrich Regiment, by the name of Conrad Pheil as sponsor. ($2.00 fee), date of the baptismal certificate 16 March 1783, Chatham.

Young von Lossberg Regiment

Anna Catharina - a legitimate daughter was born to the sergeant major of Major Baurmeister's Company, with the name Georg Henrich Reyers, and his wife, Anna Maria, nee Sadler, from Herborn, during the night between 28 and 29 January 1784, at Chatham, England, and baptized on 2 February of the same year. Anna Catharina, wife of Corporal Hermann, of the Leib Company, of the Young von Lossberg Regiment, was the sponsor. (One-half Gr[oschen]), date of the baptismal certificate 16 March 1784, Chatham.

von Donop Regiment

Andreas Maerthen - a legitimate son, was born to wedded parents in Chatham, England, on 15 February 1784. The father was a private soldier in the von Kutzleben Company, of the von Donop Regiment, by the name of Henrich Maerthen, from Zwesten, District of Borken, and the mother's name was Anna Gerdruth, born at Edeerode [Epterode ueber Witzenhausen], District of Witzenhausen. On 17 February 1784, the child was presented for baptism in the name of Jesus by the honorable member of the von Donop Regiment (von Kutzleben Company), by the name of Andreas Carteuser, born at Wernswig, District of Homburg.

Artillery

Johann Caspar Freytag - the legitimate son of the honorable artillery sergeant of the Schleestein Company, by the name of Georg Freytag, from Cassel, and his wife, Gerdruth, nee Kleinschmidt, from Melsungen, was born at Chatham, England, on 19 February 1784, at four o'clock in the afternoon, and baptized at the Royal Barracks at Chatham on the 22nd of the same month and year. Johann Caspar Katzmann, artillery servant, born at Braunhausen, District of Rothenburg, was the solicited sponsor. One-half Gr., date of the baptismal certificate 16 March 1784, Chatham.)

Confirmations

On 20 October 1782, I confirmed Elisabeth Lentz, from Volmarshausen, a legitimate daughter of Johannes Lentz, private soldier in the D'Angelelli Regiment. According to the testimony, this Elisabeth was 15 years old. She received a half-year of instruction in the Christian religion from me. I conducted this holy instruction in the Morris House, on York Island [Manhattan], in North America, in the presence of Major General von Gose and various officers of the Prince Charles Regiment.($2.00, certificate on 21 January 1786.)

Friderica Rosina Jacobi - daughter of the dead Corporal Friedrich Ludwig Jacobi, who had been in Prussian service, was born on 17 May 1770, at Koenigsberg. Her mother, Catharina Friderica, born in Ulm, was married to the soldier Christoph Stange, from Lochten, District of Finenberg, in the the Heldesheim Monastary, of the von Donop Regiment. [Friderica Rosina] was confirmed by me, in the Christian religion, on 18 March 1784, at Chatham, England.

List of Baptized Children
von Lossberg Regiment

Anna Catharina - legitimate child, born in the winter huts at Hellgate, on New York Island,, on 5 January, at four o'clock in the morning, in the year 1779; baptized on 10 January 1779. Baptismal witnesses: Conrad Hassenpflug, grenadier in the 2nd Guards Battalion, and his wife, Anna Catharina, born at Arolsen, capitol of the Principality of Waldeck. Parents: 1) Father - Johann Galenus May, gunner with the von Lossberg [Artillery] Detachment. 2) Mother - Wilhelmina Leonora, born Oberkirchen.

Von Lossberg Regiment

Sophia Wilhelmina - legitimate child, born on 21 January 1779, in the winter huts at Hellgate; baptized 24 January. Parents: 1) Father - Johann Henrich Grages, corporal in Captain von Altenbocken's Company, of the von Lossberg Regiment. 2) Mother - Dorothea Elisabeth, nee Moritz, born at Brake, in Lippe. Sponsor: Sophia Wilhelmina, wife of Corporal Haak, of the same usilier regiment.

Wilhelm Justus - legitimate child, born on York Island, in the winter huts at Hellgate, on 2 January 1779, and baptized on the 5th of the same month.

Parents: Johann Ernst Alhaus, sergeant in Colonel Scheffer's Company, of the Lossberg Regiment. The mother's name is Anna Rebecka Sehrs, a Hanoverian, from the District of Hoya. Baptismal witnesses: 1) Georg Wilhelm Helmerich, sergeant major of the above company,. 2) Johann Justus Heidmueller, corporal of the same company.

Johann Henrich - legitimate child, born 18 April 1779, at Hellgate, on New York Island, and baptized 11 April 1779. The father, named Valentin Iffert, was quartermaster sergeant of the Leib Company, of the von Lossberg Regiment. The mother was named Maria Catharina, nee Hencklein, from Bovenden. The sponsor was a field jaeger of Captain Wrede's Company, by the name of Jost Henrich Iffer, (von Lossberg Regiment.).

Baptized of the Graff Grenadier Battalion

Anna Christina - legitimate child, born 27 February 1779, and baptized 4 March of the same year. Baptism and birth were on Staten Island. Father: Georg Thiel, grenadier in Captain Hessemueller's Company. Mother: Anna Maria Sehner, born at Hausen. Sponsor: Anna Christina, nee Becker, from Zierenberg, the wife of Sergeant Schuck, of the Hessemueller Company.

Anton - legitimate child, born 6 March 1779, on Staten Island, and baptized the following day. The father was Johann Henrich Hoffer, grenadier in Captain Hohenstein's Company. Mother was Catharina Elisabeth Steuber, born in Fridewald. Sponsor was named Anton Eichenauer, of Captain Neumann's Company.

Baptisms for Other Units
Ansbach Jaeger Corps

Friedrich Henrich - illegitimate child, born to Sally Thomson, daughter of Mr. Thomson, a resident of Philadelphia. The father supposedly is Captain Christoph Friedrich von Waldenfels, commander of the Princely Ansbach Jaeger Corps. The infant was born to the world on 9 June 1779, not far from Kingsbridge, in America, and baptized 5 July 1779. Sponsor was Captain Johann Friedrich Henrich Lorey, chief of a company of the Illustrious Hessian Field Jaeger Corps. Baptismal witnesses were Captain [Justus Friedrich] Venator, of the von Donop Regiment, and Lieutenant von Ebenauer, of the Ansbach Field Jaeger Corps. NB - The baptismal certificate was issued by the von Linsing Grenadier Battalion, 25 August 1781.

Anna Dorothea - legitimate child, born to

Elisabeth Roehrscheit, from Melsungen, presently the wife of Johann Daniel Ambrosius, non-commissioned officer in Captain von Mallet's Grenadier Company, and wagon master of the von Linsing Grenadier Battalion. The infant saw the light of the world on 3 July 1779, and was baptized on the 5th of the same month and year. Sponsor was Anna Dorothea, wife of Corporal Roehrscheit, of Captain Wach's Grenadier Company. Not far from Kingsbridge, in America.

von Bose Regiment

Johann Christian Friedrich - legitimate child, born 23 July 1779, at Fort Knyphausen, on New York Island, and baptized 26 July of the same year. Father was a private soldier of Colonel von Bischhausen's Company, of the von Bose Regiment, born at Lauben, in Saxony, and name Anton Weise. The mother was from Silesia, and named Elisabeth, nee Dietrich. Sponsor was a sergeant from Colonel von Bischhausen's Company, of the same regiment, named Johann Christian Kersting, from Hobressen, District of Salzburg, from Lengercke Grenadier Battalion.

Wilhelm Philipp - legitimate child, born 18 August 1779 in the camp on New York Island, and baptized the 20th of the same month and year. Father called Dillmann Jacob, from Zumpitz, born at

Cologne, and at the time, grenadier in Captain von Gall's Company. Mother called Anna Rosina Scheurl, from Hirschfeld, Sponsor Captain von Gall, chief of the Grenadier Company of the von Donop Regiment.

von Linsing Grenadier Battalion

Catharina Elisabeth - legitimate child, was born on York Island, on 22 August 1779, and baptized on the 23rd of the same month and year. The father was a grenadier of Captain von Mallet's Company, of the Linsing Battalion, by the name of Johannes Schuetz, from Rothenburg. The mother was Anna Maria Muenster, from Wippershain [District of Hersfeld.] Sponsor Catharina Elisabeth was the wife of Grenadier Roth, of the von Linsing Battalion.

von Bose Regiment

Anna Gerdruth - legitimate child, born 29 August 1779, on New York Island, and baptized 3 September of the same year. The father was Conrad Hund, born at Langenthal, District of Helmershausen, and a private soldier in Major Dupuy's Company of the von Bose Regiment. The name of the mother was Martha Catharina, born at the same place. Sponsor Anna Gertruth Flachshaar, from Hofgeismar, wife of Sergeant [Wilhelm] Flachshaar, of the von Bose Regiment, The sergeant held the child in the name of

his wife, for the baptism.
Von Bose Regiment
Philippus - legitimate son, was born on New York Island, on 10 September 1779, and baptized by me on the 19th of the same month and year. The father was Conrad Mohr, drummer in Major Dupuy's Company, of the von Bose Regiment. The mother was Barbara Elisabeth, daughter of Gerhard Trinketrug, from Witzenhausen. Sponsor was Philipp Hunold, servant for Senior Surgeon Amelung, of the Prince Charles Regiment.

von Donop Regiment
Conrad, - legitimate son, was born on 23 September [1779?], on New York Island, and baptized the 26th of the same month and year. The father was a private soldier in Colonel Hinte's Company, of the von Donop Regiment, by the name of Henrich Bierhenne. The mother was Anna Martha, nee Wiegandt, from Falkenberg, District of Homberg. Conrad Scheffer, non-commissioned officer of the same company was the sponsor. (Baptismal certificate issued 28 October 1783. The mother went with her second husband, Doenstaedt, a non-commissioned officer, discharged by the von Donop Regiment, to Nova Scotia.)

Prince Charles Regiment

Johannes - legitimate child, born on New York Island, in the Fort Laurel Hills on 16 October 1779, and baptized on the 18th of the same month and year. The father was Wilhelm Scheffer, born at Cassel, a cannoneer with the detachment of the Prince Charles Regiment, of Captain Schleestein's Company. The mother was Maria Wilhelmina Hancken, born at Korbach, in the Principality of Waldeck. Sponsor Johannes Ostheim, born at Guntershausen, District of Cassel, was also a cannoneer of the same detachment and company.

von Donop Regiment

Anna Catharina - legitimate child, born in winter quarters at Buchwick, on Long Island, on 22 November 1779, and baptized on the 28th of the same month and year. The father was the sergeant major of Colonel von Gose's Company, called Henrich Reinhard Roem. The mother was Martha Elisabeth Vanmueller, born at Homberg, in Hesse. Anna Catharina Ritberger, born in Jesberg, wife of Musketeer Wilhelm Schroeder, of Major von Wurmb's Company, was the sponsor.

Hereditary Prince Regiment

Catharina Charlotta - an illegitimate child, was born at New York, on 7 September 1779, and at the request of Lieutenant [Carl Friedrich] Fuehrer, baptized by me on 13 January 1780. The mother, a pleasant young girl, whose fate touched me, was named Cornelia, daughter of Mr. Bayeux, a citizen of New York. She claimed the father was Lieutenant [Louis] Descourdes, of the Hereditary Prince Regiment. He had caused her downfall with a promise of marriage - nothing new in America, unfortunately. (In 1783 the father took his discharge, married the girl, and went to Nova Scotia.)

von Lossberg Regiment

Wilhelmina Leonora - the legitimate daughter of Fusilier Friedrich Conrad Achmeyer, born at Deckbergen, District of Schaumberg, was born to the world on 1 February 1780 in Herricks, on Long Island, and baptized by me on the 6th of the same month and year. The sponsor was Wilhelmina Leonora, wife of Cannoneer Galenus May, born in Obernkirchen, in the Earldom of Schaumberg.

von Lossberg Regiment

Annette Luzie Margaretha - legitimate daughter, was born to Fusilier Georg Henrich Fock, of Colonel Scheffer's Company, of the von Lossberg Regiment, born at Guntersblum, in the Earldom of Leiningen, and his wife, Maria Catharina Leisner, born at Weinelsen, in the Pfalz, at Herricks, on Long

Island, on 30 December 1779, was baptized by me there, on 6 February 1780. The sponsor was Annette Luzie Margaretha, wife of Fusilier [Johannes] Trautwein of the same company and regiment.

Andreas - an illegitimate son, was born at New York, on 17 April 1780, to Barbara Rheider, born at Rhode Island, and the daughter of an Anabaptist by the name of Rheider. The mentioned Barbara said Lieutenant Dietzel, of the Hessian Artillery was the father, and added that she had had a child by him previously, which was still living. NB - She calls herself Mrs. Dietzel, because, she says, her marriage was made in Heaven. A soldier of the Leib Company, of the von Donop Regiment, named Adam Zuelch, was the sponsor on 20 April 1780, at New York. Therefore, another pair of wretched boys and girls more in the world.

Therefore, take care and do not be fooled
By a man who promises to marry you.
(NB - Father and child died in New York in 1781.)

von Buenau Regiment

Johanna Margaretha - was born on Staten Island, on 4 May 1780, and baptized on the 7th of the same month and year. The father was a non-commissioned officer of the Leib Company of the von Buenau Garrison Regiment, by the name of

Franz Christoph Mangold, born at Eschwege. The mother was from the same place, and named Anna Catharina, nee Gebhard. The two were legally married. Johanna Margaretha, wife of Conrad Grosz, cannoneer of the Leib Company, of the Artillery Corps was the sponsor.

1780

Elisabeth Christina - a daughter, was born to Georg Adolph Frey, born at Groszenkeder, in the Schwarzenburg, (servant to Major General von Gose), and his wife, Anna Margaretha, nee Rosenthal, from Vacha, on 11 September 1780, at New York, and baptized on the 14th of the same month and year. The sponsor was Elizabeth Christina, nee Brand, wife of Fusilier Friedrich Huether, of the Hereditary Prince Regiment. (Died 18 September of the same year.)

Leib Regiment

Johann Valentin - the legitimate son of Cannoneer David Eberhard, from Cassel, of Captain Schleestein's Artillery Company, and his wife, Dorothea Elisabeth Tippel, also born at Cassel, was born at New York on 19 September 1780, and baptized there on the 24th of the same month and year. The sponsor was Valentin Humburg, gunsmith of the Leib Regiment, also born at Cassel.

HESSIAN CHAPLAINS

General Staff

Maria Elisabeth - daughter of the Hessian Provisions' Administrator, by the name of Johannes Ebert, born at Wabern, in the District of Homberg, and his wife, Maria Elisabeth, nee Pelotrow, from New York, in America, was born at New York on 2 October 1780, and baptized by me at the request of both parents, on the 13th of the same month and year. The mother, herself, acted as the sponsor, and the baptismal witness was a good friend of theirs by the name of Samuel Comphiel, a citizen and resident of New York. NB - This Maria Elisabeth, wife of the Provisions' Administrator Ebert, was confirmed at New York on 25 September 1780, after being instructed by me for a period of eight weeks in the Reformed religion.

von Linsing Grenadier Battalion, 1780-1781

Johannes Franziscus - legitimate son of Grenadier Christoph Holzmueller, of Captain von Mallet's Company, of the von Linsing Grenadier Battalion, born at Bovenden, and his wife Dorothea Claus, also from Bovenden, was born on 19 December 1780, in the camp at Jamaica, on Long Island, and baptized by me on the 20th of the same month and year. The sponsor was Johannes

Franziscus Gottlob, grenadier of the same company, born at Wuerzburg. NB - A Catholic.

von Roeder Jaeger Company
Ansbach Service

Philipp Adam - legitimate son of Christian Conrad Rummel, field jaeger in Ansbach service, born in Ansbach, and in Captain von Roeder's Company, and his wife, Margaretha Barbara Rincks, also born in Ansbach, was born at Flushing, on Long Island, on 18 January 1781, and baptized by me on the 20th of the same month and year. Sponsor was Philipp Adam Wenig, private jaeger in Captain von Waldenfels' Company, also in Ansbach service.

Von Linsing Grenadier Battalion, 1781

Johannes - legitimate son of Grenadier Gerhard Fuellgraff, born at Epterode, District of Witzenhausen, and his wife, Anna Gerdruth, nee Schick, of Epterode, was born on 11 February 1781 at Jamaica on Long Island, and baptized on the 13th of the same month and year. Sponsor Johannes Schuetz, grenadier of the same company, was born at Rotenburg.

1781

Eva Elisabeth - was born on 17 March 1781, at Herricks, on Long Island, and baptized on the 21st of the same month and year. She was the legitimate daughter of a mounted jaeger of Lieutenant Colonel von Wurmb's Company, by the name of Caspar Schmid, born at Ulfen, District of Sontra, and his wife, Anna Maria, nee Humburg, from Crumbach, District of Cassel. The sponsor was Eva Elisabeth, wife of the mounted jaeger Koerbel.

1781, von Donop Regiment

Maria Amelia - legitimate daughter of Hautboist Johann Ludwig Schmidt, of the von Donop Regiment, born at Fuhlen, in the District of Oldenburg, and his wife, Maria Catharina, nee Brandenburg, from Hausbergen, not far from Prussian-Muenden, was born on Long Island during the afternoon of 13 April, and baptized on the 15th of the same month and year, Otto Friedrich Krueschel, sergeant major of Major von Wurmb's Company, was the sponsor, in his wife Maria Amalia's name. NB - The mother died on [blank] September 1781, of [Slux]. The child was placed in a nursery at our cost, because the father had nothing. (The child died 2 October 1781.)

Johannes - a legitimate son of Drummer Adam Schmeck, of the Vacant Colonel's Company, of the von Donop Regiment, and his wife, Anna Martha, was born on York Island, on 18 May 1781, and baptized on the 23rd of the same month and year. Johannes Dickhaut, musketeer of the same company was the sponsor. (Mgts?)

Jaeger Corps, 1781

Dorothea Christina - the legitimate daughter of Johann Christoph Wicks, field jaeger of Captain Ewald's Company, born at Cassel, and his wife, Anna Maria, nee Losch, from Cassel, was born on Long Island on 15 June 1781, and baptized by me at Fort Knyphausen on 30 June 1781. Anna Dorothea, wife of Field Jaeger Friedrich Apt, of the same company, was sponsor.

von Donop Regiment

Johann Henrich - legitimate son of Joachim Kurz, musketeer (of Major von Kutzleben's Company), of the von Donop Regiment, and his wife, Anna Catharina, nee Viemann, of Zimmersrode, was born on 1 July 1781, at Fort Kynphausen, and baptized on the 5th of the same month and year. Sponsor was Musketeer Johann Henrich Schmidt, of the same company.

Jaeger Corps Barracks
At Fort Knyphausen (Prussian)

Johann Adam - legitimate son of Field Jaeger

Michael Rupport, of Captain Ewald's Company, born at Aschaffenburg, and his wife, Regina, nee Brand, from Wurm, born 20 July 1781, on York Island, and baptized by me, on the 23rd of the same month and year. Sponsor was the gunsmith of the Jaeger Corps, Johann Adam Pfaff. Catholic.

Jaeger Corps, 1781

Johannes - legitimate son of Christian Lockberger, Hessian field jaeger in Captain von Donop's Company, born at Jena, and his wife, Anna Christina, nee Schreiber, from Seligenthal, by Schmalkalden, was born at Fort Knyphausen, on New York Island, on 10 August 1781, and baptized on the 15th of the same month and year. His baptismal sponsor was Johannes Ulrich, musketeer in the Prince Charles Regiment.

von Loewenstein Grenadier Battalion

Anna Catharina - was born in the camp at McGowan's Pass, on New York Island, on 22 August 1781, at four o'clock in the morning, (so I am told), and baptized by me on the 23rd of the same month and year. The father was Nicolaus Boulanger, born at Markirch, in Lothringen, grenadier in the von Ditfurth Grenadier Company, Captain [Friedrich] Klingender, of the von Loewenstein Battalion. The mother was Christina, nee May, of Treysa, in the District of

Ziegenhain, The sponsor was Anna Catharina Mentzler, widow of the dead Grenadier Jacob Mentzler, from Frankenburg.

Squadron

Daniel Heinbeck - was born on 1 September 1781, in the Jaeger camp at Kingsbridge on New York Island, and baptized by me on the 6th of the same month and year. The father was Johannes Stephan Heinbeck, a private jaeger in the von Wurmb Squadron, born at Sohl, in Electoral Saxony. Anna Catharina, nee Kaufhold, from Grossalmerode, was the mother. Corporal Daniel Selzam, of the von Wurmb Squadron, was the sponsor.

Artillery Detachment with the Jaeger Corps

Eva - daughter of Sergeant Gottfried Kip, of Lieutenant Colonel Eitel's Artillery Company, born at Dittershausen, in the District of Cassel-Neustadt, and his wife, Martha Catharina, nee Vogeley, born in Allendorf, was born in the Jaeger Camp at Kingsbridge, on 7 September 1781, and baptized by me at that time. The sponsor was Eva, wife of Artillery Servant Katzmann, of Captain Schleestein's Company, serving with the von Donop Regiment.

Jaeger Corps, 1781

Rosina - a legitimate child, was born on New York Island, in the Jaeger Camp below Fort Tryon, on 17 September 1781. Her father, Peter Paul Wirths, private jaeger of Lieutenant Colonel von Prueschenck's Company, was born at Bonn, in Cologne. Gerdruth nee Schumacher, from Nastaetten, by Rheinfels, was the mother. The day of the holy rebirth of the newborn child, was 19 September 1781, when Rosina, nee Ulrich, from Colmar, presently the wife of Corporal Seidling, of Major von Wurmb's Jaeger Company, was the requested sponsor.

Squadron

Johanna Rosina Justina - a legitimate child, was born to the world on 26 September 1781, on York Island, near the Morris House. Her father, Eusebrius Eremeteich Henschel, born at Krumhendersdorf, in Electoral Saxony, is presently a mounted jaeger in Lieutenant Colonel von Wurmb's Company. Anna Barbara, nee Orthwein, from Marburg, was the mother. The child was baptized on the 28th, when Rosina, nee Ulrich, from Colmar, wife of Corporal Seidling (of Major von Wurmb's Company), and the Jaeger's gunsmith, Johann Adam Pfaff, were the requested sponsors.

Prince Charles Regiment

Johann Georg Frey - legitimate son of Georg Adolph Frey, born at Groszenkeder, in the Schwarzenburg, presently the servant of Major General Baron von Gose. The mother of the newly-born was Margaretha, nee Rosenthal, from Vacha. According to the statement, the child was born on 6 October 1781, at four P.M., on York Island, at the so-called Reed House. Upon request, I baptized it on 17 October 1781, with Johann Georg Wagner, servant of His Excellency, Lieutenant General von Knyphausen, as sponsor.

von Donop Regiment

Anna Elisabeth - legitimate daughter of Johannes Scheffer, soldier in Colonel Heymel's Company, and his wife, Anna Elisabeth, nee Hars, from Roemersberg, District of Borken, was born on 11 January 1782, at seven P.M., at Marsten's Wharf on York Island, and baptized on the 15th of the same month and year. Johannes Emloth, musketeer of Colonel Heymel's Company, born at Roemersberg, held the child to be baptized in the name of his sister, Anna Elisabeth Emloth.

von Donop Regiment

Anna Elisabeth - a daughter was born to Philipp Guembell, of Major von Kutzleben's Company, and his wife, Anna Elisabeth, nee Pflueger, from Homberg, in Hesse, was born between five and six A.M., on 13 January 1782, on York Island, not far from Murphy's House, and baptized on the 15th. A soldier of the same company, named Conrad Opfer, of Hebel, District of Homberg, held the child for baptism, in the name of the father's sister, Anna Elisabeth Guembell, from Oberurff-Schiffelborn.

von Donop Regiment

Henrich Reinhard Dickhaut - legitimate son, was born on New York Island, not far from Marsten's Wharf, on the East River, on 25 February 1782,. His father was a musketeer in the Leib Company, of the said regiment, named Werner Dickhaut, born at Holzhausen, in the District of Homberg. The mother, Anna Gerdruth, nee Pickhard, was also from Holzhausen. The newborn was baptized on the 29th of the same month and year. Sergeant Major Henrich Reinhard Roem, of Colonel Heymel's Company, was the sponsor.

[Artillery] Detachment
With the Prince Charles Regiment

Elisabeth Scheffer - a legitimate child, was born on 8 February 1782, about five P.M., at McGowan's Pass, on York Island, and on the 10th of the same month and year, baptized by me, by request. Wilhlem

Scheffer, born at Cassel, cannoneer in Captain Schleestein's Company, was the father, and his wife, Maria Wilhelmina, nee Hanck, of Korbach, in the Principality of Waldeck, was the mother. Elizabeth, wife of the soldier Eichler, of Colonel von Lengercke's Company, of the Prince Charles Regiment, was the sponsor. NB - The sponsor was from Philippsthal, District of Vacha.

Von Donop Regiment

Anna Catharina - a legitimate daughter, was born to the world on 12 February 1782, near the city of New York, and on the 17th of the same month and year, baptized by me. Christoph Stange, from Lochtum, District of Vienenburg, Monastary Hildesheim, presently musketeer in Major von Wurmb's Company, of the von Donop Regiment, was the father. Catharina Friederica, born at Ulm, was the mother. Anna Catharina, wife of Musketeer Georg Schroeder, of the same company, was the sponsor. (dd baptismal certificate in March 1784.)

Names of those I have Confirmed
In my Role as Chaplain

On Easter, 31 March 1777, I confirmed two lads, who had already been taken on by the Minnigerode Battalion, as fifers. Both were children with good spirits and healthy intellects. I had instructed them in religion for nine weeks, and never worked with greater pleasure than with these children. I easily gave then the basis for our religion, allowing them to memorize some - and how supple the human heart can be, when a person has found the right way! They learned the words of consolation from the Bible, and also the five chief articles, without being forced to do so by me. "It is good for you," I often said, "my children. It will give you courage in danger, and consolation in death, if you also keep it in mind." That is what I said, and those few words, were enough to impress their tender souls. They gave me great pleasure here. How great it will be in the hereafter. May my future students give me the joy, which these first ones gave me! The older was Johannes Krueck, born at Rinteln, in 1763. His father was a grenadier in Captain von Wilmowsky's Company, named Henrich Krueck. The other [nothing more added].

On 19 May 1779, I confirmed a youth of Captain von Alten-Bockum's Company, of the von

Lossberg Fusilier Regiment, at New York. His name was Friedrich Heidenrich. He was born at Rinteln and was 14 years old.

On 10 May 1780, I confirmed a young girl, 13 years old, at New York, in the presence of her parents. Her name was Anna Elisabeth Gleim, born at Melsungen, on the Fulda. The father was Johannes Gleim, born at Hersfeld, and a fifer in Captain von Mallet's Grenadier Company, of the von Mirbach Regiment. The mother, Elisabeth, Pflueger, was born at Rotenburg. NB - This girl gave me much pleasure, not only because of her eagerness to learn, but also, because of her outward decorum, not a little joy.

Martha Elisabeth Schaeffer - from Harle, District of Flensberg, who was confirmed by Chaplain Kuemmell, at Rhode Island, in 1778. Because she could show no confirmation testimonial, was privately examined, and based on the remarks of her then master, the master-baker Ostwald, of New York, she was admitted to the sacrament. Certificate issued on 12 May 1780. NB - The parents are: father: Henrich Schaeffer, sergeant in the von Huyn Regiment - mother: Anna Elisabeth, nee Ditmar, from Singlis, District of Borken. Comment - Chaplain Kuemmell was at Charleston with the von Huyn Regiment at that time.

On the second Easter Day, that is 1 April 1782, I confirmed Friedrich Almeroth, born at Homberg, in Hesse, in March 1768, after he gained the proper knowledge of the Christian religion, following his having reached his 14th year, in an open assembly at Marsten's Wharf, on the Island of New York. The father was the captain-at-arms of the Leib Company, of the von Donop Regiment, by the name of Georg Almeroth. The mother Egidia Almeroth, born at Hersfeld.

Supplement
On 9 September 1778, I was asked by a friend to baptize the five-day old child of an inhabitant on Long Island, because the pastor had joined the rebels. I made some objection, because I had not acquired sufficient proficiency in the English language to make myself understood to the people. However, the persistent entreaties of the parents overcame my objections. I went there and baptized the child according to our practice, with the regimental surgeon in attendance. The child was a girl. The sponsor was named Elisabeth Plaumens, and named it Merry [Mary?].

The father was a poor shoemaker, named Thomas Pauer; the mother, Isabella Pauuer. The place where they lived was a pleasant and lively little village directly opposite New York, by the name of Brooklyn Ferry. Father and mother wept for joy over their good fortune, that now their beloved child had been taken into the Christian fold, by the bond of baptism. They spoke continuous praises for me. And, as they had nothing else with which to show their appreciation, I had to drink a half-glass of wine with the woman who had just had the delivery. Long Island, in the camp at Brooklyn Ferry, 9 September 1776. (Cannon Beach)

- - - - - - -

[A small poem]
Glory, wealth, splendor, the concerns of the
court,
Adored by the people,
Are not worth the efforts of men of the earth

- - - - - - -

[Another poem]
To a Sad Friend
My dear friend,
Do not let sorrow and fear,
The destroyers of courage, overcome you!

You live for pleasure.
Why let the old worries create new problems?
Remain true to the eloquence of Heaven!
In that way

HESSIAN CHAPLAINSH

You will soon overcome envy,
And suppress disgrace and slander.

Note how the eagle does it,
Which suddenly grasps a viper
That ventures out of the bushes.
He fights with might,
And rises high in the air with it,
Tears it apart with his claws,
And swallows it down,
And flies in serene calm,
As before, in the sky.
- - - - - - -

[Here the official entries of Chaplain Coester end. Unfortunately, no personal comments concerning his stay in America are known to exist.]

Chaplain Braundorff's

ANHALT-ZERBST CHURCH BOOK

HESSIAN CHAPLAINS

Church Book
Kept for the Troops of the Ruler of Anhalt-Zerbst In the Service of the King of England Containing the Record of Deaths, [Births], Baptisms, and Marriages Beginning 21 February 1778, the Day of their Departure from Zerbst By M. Johann Gottlieb Siegismund Braunsdorf, Chaplain

Translated and transcribed by Bruce E. Burgoyne

- - - - - - - -

Introduction

Locked safely away in the Evangelical-Lutheran Church Archives in Jever, Germany, there is a document, which has seldom seen the light of day, and which is rapidly losing its value to either the German or the American people. The document is the church book, which according to the title, was used to record deaths, [births], baptisms, and marriages of the Anhalt-Zerbst soldiers, who served England during the American Revolutionary War. However, only the deaths are listed [?] in the Old German script, and the entries, such as reference to Pointe-Levi as Pointe-Lewis, clearly indicate that the document was prepared after the soldiers had returned to Germany.

HESSIAN CHAPLAINS

Nevertheless, the document is of significance as it provides a deeper understanding of the tragedy of war and the common bond of death, which men, women, and children, of all nations face daily.

I know of no battles fought by the men of Anhalt-Zerbst, one of the six petty German states, which provided the "Hessians", but one soldier from Anhalt-Zerbst was captured while on guard at Paulus Hook, in New Jersey. Still, the Church Book kept by Chaplain Johann Gottlieb Siegismund Braunsdorf lists 165 men, women, and children of the Anhalt-Zerbst contingent who died, from the time it left its home area in 1778, until early 1785, after the return to Germany.

In addition to an English translation, I have made a typed transcription of the German [not published] as the Old German script is no longer taught to German school children. The English translation will enable American students who are not fluent in German, to more easily learn something of the men whose activity had a bearing on our nation's founding. My transcription contains errors but I have done the best that I could with a handwriting, which sometimes degenerated into a near-meaningless scrawl, which I dropped completely, in most cases. It will be readily apparent that the same individuals' names were even spelled differently at times, and sometimes I could only guess at the spelling of proper names. I have used a letter e after vowels a, o, and u to indicate umlauts Also some numbers have a sub-letter suffix, which I could not decipher in many cases, and in others made only a guess. In making the translation, I have taken certain liberties in altering sentence and phrasing structure to make a more readable document. As always, I recommend that serious students go back to the document that I worked from, in order to verify my transcription and/or translation.

I have translated some forty or more of the German-language documents written by the participants in the American Revolution, but nothing previously done has the poignancy of this simple document, in which are recorded the loss of fathers, mothers, children, husbands, and other relatives, not as a result of combat, but just due to the daily hardships of military life. While most of the deaths were probably due to illness, the book records deaths during and following childbirth, accidents, and too many suicides.

Georg Janssen - Sillenstede has previously published an edited version of this church book in the <u>Oldenburg Jahrbuch</u> parts 44/45, Oldenburg Edition, 1940/41, but his article listed only the soldiers. By *neglecting to include the wives and children, he left out the heart of the document, and deprived descendants of that sympathy and compassion, which even our "enemies" are entitled to receive.*

Finally, I must thank the pastor and personnel of the Church Office in Jever for providing me with a copy of Chaplain Braunsdorf's Church Book, so that I could make this information available to present-day readers.

Dover, DE, December 1991   *Bruce E. Burgoyne*

HESSIAN CHAPLAINS

Death Register for the Year 1778
Death Register for March 1778

- - - - - - - -

1. Johann Berges died on 16 March, on the march to Lamspringe, in Hildesheim. He was the provost for the Anhalt-Zerbst contingent, and of the Evangelical faith. His age was unknown.

2. Wilhelm Dietrich Fuchs died on 16 April at Stade, in Hannover. He belonged to Captain Gogel's Company. Born at Jever, he was of the Evangelical faith, and had served in the Anhalt-Zerbst forces 3 years and 2 months. His age was 22 years, 4 months, and 3 days.

3. Johann Crass died on 26 April aboard the ship *Sally*, and was buried near Glueckstadt, in Denmark. [Glueckstadt is now in Germany.] He belonged to Colonel von Rauschenplat's Company. Born in Mainz, he was of the Catholic faith, and a wigmaker by trade. He had served 2 years and 8 months in the military, and was 42 years old.

4. Heinrich Harms died on 12 May aboard the ship *The Rising Sun*, and was buried on shore near Portsmouth, England. A member of Captain Piquet's Grenadier Company, he had been born at Jever, was of the Evangelical faith, and was married, having left a son and three daughters behind. He had been in

Anhalt-Zerbst service since 27 April 1766. He was 34 years old.

5. Peter Schroeder died on 12 May aboard the ship *Wisk*, and was buried the next day, near Portsmouth. Born at Werpen, in Anhalt-Zerbst, he was a member of Captain Prince of Schwarz-burg's Company. He was of the Evangelical faith, and had served 3 months. He was 22 years old.

6. Gottfried Knaust died on 19 May aboard the *Wisk*, at Portsmouth, and was buried on land. Born at Gratenhanchen, in Saxony. He belonged to Captain Prince of Schwarzburg's Company, and was of the Evangelical faith. He had served 3 months and 2 weeks, and was 20 years old.

7. Ehrhardt Caspar died on 27 May on board *The Rising Sun*, en route to the harbor at Torbay, England, and was buried on land at that place. Born at Jever, he belonged to Captain Gogel's Company. He was married and left a wife and child behind in Jever. On 30 January 1762 he had entered the Anhalt-Zerbst service. He was of the Evangelical faith, and 50 years old.

8. Ludewich Hennig died on 28 May aboard the *Antelope* in the harbor at Torbay, where he was buried on land. A member of Captain von Wietersheim's Company, he had been born at Zerbst, and was of the

Evangelical faith. He hasd served 6 years, 11 months, and was 19 years old.

9. Christian Koenig died on 2 June on the *Wisk* in the harbor at Torbay, where he was buried. Born at Ferthen, in Saxony, he was of the Evangelical faith, and a member of Captain Prince of Schwarzburg's Company. He was a baker by trade, and had served in the military since 2 September 1777.

10. August Balle died on 7 June on the ship *Sally* in the harbor at Torbay, where he was buried. Born in Zerbst, he was of the Evangelical faith and a member of Captain Piquet's Grenadier Company. He had been in service since 21 April 1775, and was 26 years old.

11. Heinrich Ihnen died on 17 June on the *Wisk*, from which he was buried in the ocean. Born at Jever, he was of the Evangelical faith, and a member of Major von Rauschenplat's Company. He was a linen-weaver by trade, and was married, having left a wife and three daughters behind. He had served for 2 years, and was 39 years old.

12. Erdmann Mueller died on 25 June on the *Present Succession,* and was buried at sea. Born at Groebzig, in Dessau, he was of the Evangelical faith, and a member of Colonel von Rauschen-plat's Company. He had served a year and one-half, and was 21 years old.

13. Wilhelm Hinderichs died on 27 July, on the *Antelope*, and was buried at sea. He was from Sollenstad, in Jever, of the Evangelical faith, and a member of Captain von Wietersheim's Grenadier Company. He had been in service 2 years, and left a wife behind in Jever. He was 25 years old.

14. Gottlieb Raebels died on 27 July on the *Present Succession*, and was buried at sea. Born in Zerbst, he was of the Evangelical faith, and a member of Captain Prince of Schwarzburg's Company. He had been in service since 18 August 1774, and was 20 years old.

15. Gottfried Piltz died on 12 August, on the ship *Sally*. He was born in Zerbst, was of the Evangelical faith, and a member of Colonel von Rauschenplat's Company. A cloth maker by trade, who had served in the military since 12 July 1773, he left a wife behind. He was 25 years old.

16. Jost Heinrich Stahlbuck died on 20 August on *The Rising Sun*, and was buried at sea. He was born in Jever, and of the Evangelical faith. He was a member of Captain Gogel's Company, and had been in service for 30 years. He left a wife and son behind in Jever. He was 50 years old.

17a. Anna Catharina Coje, nee List, died 26 August on the *Antelope*, and was buried on land the next day. She was the wife of Grenadier Adam Coje, of Captain von Wietersheim's Company, and had been born at Dessau, at the Red Estate. Her father, a day laborer by the name of Christopher List, is still living. She was 25 years old.

18x. Carolina Sophia Margaretha Andress died on 31 August, after being baptized in an emergency ceremony on *The Rising Sun*, and was buried on land. She was the 1 day-old daughter of Grenadier Christian Andress, of Captain Piquet's Company.

19. Bernhard Duittgen died on 4 September on *The Rising Sun,* while sailing in the St. Lawrence River, and was buried two days later on land. He was of the Evangelical faith, married, and left a wife and daughter behind. He had served in the Anhalt-Zerbst military for 40 years, and was 65 years old.

20. Heinrich Sunder died on 4 September on the *Present Succession*, and was buried on land. Born in Oldenburg, he was a member of Captain Gogel's Company, and had served in the military for 3 years. He was of the Evangelical faith, and left his wife and a daughter behind in Jever. He was 30 years old.

21. Reinhardt Moos died 5 September on board the *Wisk*, and was buried on land. Born Busenkirsel Parish, in Oldenburg, he was of the Evangelical faith, and a member of Major von Rauschenplat's Company. He was 28 years old.

22b. Mrs. Brandt, wife of Private Andreas Brandt, of Captain Gogel's Company, died 8 September as she was about to debark from *The Rising Sun*, and was buried at Quebec. She had been born at Grathin, was of the Evangelical faith, and was 35 years old.

23c. Barbara Henckelmann, daughter of Private Veit Henckelmann, of Major von Rauschenplat's Company, died on the *Wisk* on 29 August. She was 1 year and 6 months old.

24. Jacob Flammer, of Captainn Prince of Schwarzburg's Company, died in the hospital Hotel de Dieu, at Quebec, on 10 September, and was buried in the English cemetery there. He was born at Eschelbrunn, in Wuerttenberg, was of the Evangelical faith, and was a stocking maker by trade. He had been

in service since 23 May 1777, and was 16 years old.

25. Martin Koehler born Gommern, in Saxony, died on 11 September, in the hospital Hotel de Dieu, at Quebec. A member of Captain Piquet's Grenadier Company, he had served in the military since 2 December 1769. He was of the Evangelical faith, and 27 years old.

26. Johann Preiss, from the Tyrol, died on 11 September, in the hospital Hotel de Dieu, at Quebec. He was a member of Captain Piquet's Grenadier Company, and had previously served the King of France for 9 years. He was of the Catholic faith, a mason by trade, and had served in the Anhalt-Zerbst military since 5 September 1775. He was 40 years old.

27. Johann Oelrichs, born in Jever, died on 12 September in the hospital Hotel de Dieu, at Quebec. A member of Captain Piquet's Grenadier Company, and a carpenter by trade, he was of the Evangelical faith, and had been in service since 16 July 1774. He was 21 years old.

28. Ulrich Gerdes, a corporal in the Anhalt-Zerbst Artillery Corps, died in the hospital Hotel de Dieu, at Quebec, on 12 September. Born at Jever, of the Evangelical faith, he was a tailor by trade, and had served in the military for 14 years. His age was

unknown.

29.   Heinrich Fischer, born at Seiferode in Darmstadt, died on 13 September in the general hospital at Quebec, and was buried in the Protestant portion of the cemetery, at that place. He belonged to Colonel von Rauschenplat's Company, was of the Evangelical faith, and a tailor by trade. He was 19 years and 8 months old.

30. The Gunsmith Dieterich for the Anhalt-Zerbst contingent died on 16 September in the general hospital at Quebec, where he was buried. He had been born at Pautzen, was of the Evangelical faith, and had left a wife behind at Zerbst. He was 34 years old.

31. Gottfried Grachelitz, of the Jaeger Corps, fell to his death from the window of the uppermost floor of the barracks on 16 September. Born Basen, in Schweidnitz, he was of the Evangelical faith, and a trained hunter. He was 30 years old.

32.   Heinrich Rinkler, of Captain Piquet;s Grenadier Company, died on 16 September, in the hospital Hotel de Dieu, at Quebec. He was from Nassau-Weilburg, of the Evangelical faith, and a roof-slater by trade. He had served in the military since 25 February 1775, and was 24 years old.

33,   Carl Daniel, of Captain Piquet's Grenadier Company, died 18 September in the hospital Hotel de

HESSIAN CHAPLAINS

Dieu, at Quebec. Born at Muehlhausen, in Wuerzburg, he had served 2 and ¼ years in Wuerzburg military service previously, and had entered Anhalt-Zerbst service on 12 July 1775. He was of the Catholic faith, and was 25 years old.

34. Johann Neuhaus died 18 September in the hospital Hotel de Dieu, at Quebec. He belonged to Captain Piquet's Grenadier Company, and had served since 6 January 1778, in the Anhalt-Zerbst military.

35. Christopher Hoyer, 1st sergeant in Captain Piquet's Grenadier Company, died on 19 September in the hospital Hotel de Dieu, at Quebec. Born in Dessau, he had left his wife and a son and daughter behind in Coswig. He was of the Evangelical faith, and had served in the military since 8 November 1768. He was 24 years old.

36s. Johann Gottlieb Brandt, a small son of Private And. Brandt, of Captain Gogel's Company, died 20 September, in the barracks at Quebec. He had been born on 28 December 1777, at Zerbst.

37. Gottfried Haucke, 1st sergeant of Colonel von Rauschenplat's Company, died 27 September, in the hospital Hotel de Dieu, at Quebec. Born in Zerbst, and of the Evangelical faith, he left a wife behind in Zerbst. He was 36 years old.

38. Matthias Schussler, assistant surgeon of the

Anhalt-Zerbst contingent, died on 27 September, in the hospital Hotel de Dieu, at Quebec. Born in Barby, and of the Evangelical faith, he had been in service since 16 January 1777. He was 28 years old.

39. Christoph Tiarks, Sr., a cannoneer in the Artillery Corps, died on 28 September in the hospital Hotel de Dieu, at Quebec. Born at Jever, and of the Evangelical faith, he left a wife, a son, and a daughter behind in Jever. He had been in service for 9 years, and was 32 years old.

40. Christian Ruehling, of Colonel von Rauschenplat's Company, died on 29 September in the hospital Hotel de Dieu, at Quebec. He was born in Blankenburg, in Brunswick, and had previously served in the Brunswick Leib [Body] Regiment. He was of the Evangelical faith. He entered Anhalt-Zerbst service at Stade, and was 31 years old.

41. Wilhelm Schoenholz, of Captain Prince of Schwarzburg's Company, died in the hospital Hotel de Dieu, at Quebec, on 29 September. Born in Zerbst, he was of the Evangelical faith, and a shoemaker by trade. He was 18 years old.

42. Jacob Ferber, born at Westheim, in Electoral Pfalz, died 29 September, in the general hospital at Quebec. A member of Colonel von Rauschernplat's Company, he was of the Catholic faith, and 23 years

old.

43. Johann Georg Wilhelm von Zawadsky, corporal in the Anhalt-Zerbst Jaeger Corps, died 1 October, in the hospital Hotel de Dieu, at Quebec. Born at Zahne, in Wittenberg, he was a trained hunter, and had entered the military service on 30 October 1777. He was 27 years old.

44. Christian Bergholz, a drummer in Captain Piquet's Grenadier Company, died 3 October, in the hospital Hotel de Dieu, at Quebec. Born in Roslau, in Anhalt-Zerbst, he was of the Evangelical faith, and had entered service on 9 October 1775. He was 14 years old.

45d. Christian Wenzel, the small son of Private Daniel Wenzel, of Captain Prince of von Schwarzburg's Company, died 3 October in the barracks at Quebec. He had been born 4 February 1776, at Arnstadt, in Schwarzburg-Sondershausen.

46. Tobias Thiem, cannoneer in the Artillery Corps, died 4 October in the hospital Hotel de Dieu, at Quebec. Born in the small settlement of Froshe, in Prussia, he was of the Evangelical faith, and left a wife and daughter behind in Jever. He was 27 years old.

47. Christoph Jahn, born at Wormstaedt, in Weimar, died 4 October in the hospital Hotel de Dieu,

at Quebec. A member of Captain von Wietersheim's Grenadier Company, he was of the Lutheran faith, and a cooper by trade. He was 30 years old.

48. Friederich Baetge, born in Magdeburg, died on 5 October, in the hospital Hotel de Dieu, at Quebec. A member of Captain Prince von Schwarzburg's Company, he was of the Lutheran faith, and a tailor by trade. He was 18 years old.

49. Adam Baumgarten, corporal in Major von Rauschenplat's Company, died on 7 October at Quebec. Born in Rodelber, near Badendurlach, he was of the Catholic faith, and 19 years old.

50. Ludewich Thuden, private in Major von Rauschenplat's Company, died 8 October in the hospital Hotel de Dieu, in Quebec. Born in Jever, he was of the Evangelical faith, and was 16 years old.

51. Abel Heyd, of Captain Gogel's Company, died on 19 October in the hospital Hotel de Dieu, at Quebec. Born in Gotha, he was of the Evangelical faith, and a mason by trade. He left a wife behind in Jever. He was 36 years old.

52f. Gottfried Thiele, jaeger in the Anhalt-Zerbst Jaeger Corps, died on 12 October in the hospital Hotel de Dieu, at Quebec. Born in Mannsfeld, he was of the Evangelical faith, and 22 years old.

53. Ludewich Koehler, private in Captain Gogel's

Company, died 12 October in the hospital Hotel de Dieu, in Quebec. Born in Klein Schmalkalden, he was of the Evangelical faith, and 40 years old.

54. Heinrich Kotenkampf, private in Colonel von Rauschenplat's Company, died 12 October in the hospital Hotel de Dieu, in Quebec. Born in Bremen, he was of the Evangelical faith, and was 17 years old.

55c. Friederich Wentzel, son of Private Daniel Wentzel, of Captain Prince of Schwarzburg's Company, died 12 October in the general hospital, at Quebec. He was 4 months [days ?] old.

56b. Margaretha Wentzelin, wife of Private Daniel Wentzel, of Captain Prince of Schwarzburg's Company, died 16 October, in the general hospital, at Quebec. Born in Nuernberg, she was 38 years old.

57 Friederich Bencke, quartermaster sergeant in Major von Rauschenplat's Company, died 20 October in the hospital Hotel de Dieu, in Quebec. Born at Sehren, in Anhalt-Zerbst. He was of the Evangelical faith, and 37 years old.

58c. Maria Catharina Brandtin, wife of Corporal Brandt, of Captain Gogel's Company, died 27 October, in the general hospital, at Quebec. Born in Coswig, in Anhalt-Zerbst, she was of the Evangelical faith, and 47 years old.

59d. Barbara Henkelmannin, wife of Private Veit

Henkelmann, of Major von Rauschenplat's Company, died 25 October, in the hospital at Quebec. Born at Germershausen, in Wuerzburg, she was of the Catholic faith, and 26 years old.

60. Georg Groneberg, private in Captain Piquet's Grenadier Company, died 29 October, in the general hospital, at Quebec. Born in Sondershausen, he was of the Evangelical faith, married, and 28 years old. . .

61. Christian Baer, fifer in Captain von Wietersheim's Grenadier Company, died on 30 October, in the hospital Hotel de Dieu, in Quebec. Born at Roslau, in Anhalt-Zerbst, he was of the Evangelical faith, and 15 years old.

62y. Maria Christiana Coje, the only daughter of Private Coje, of Captain von Wietersheim's Grenadier Company, died 30 October, in the barracks, at Quebec. She was 1 year and 9 months old.

63d. Johann Heinrich Hentze, the small son of Private Hentze, of Captain Prince of Schwarzburg's Company, died 2 November in the barracks at Quebec. He was 17 weeks old.

64. Gottfried Bleich, private in Captain Piquet's Grenadier Company, died 2 November in the hospital Hotel de Dieu, at Quebec. Born in Zerbst, he was of the Evangelical faith, and a cloth-maker by trade. He was married, and 32 years old.

65e. Maria Elisabeth Hentzin, wife of Private Hentze, of Captain Prince of Schwarzburg's Company, died 3 November in the general hospital in Quebec. Born in the monastery at Hildesheim, she was of the Evangelical faith, and 35 years old.

66. Ludewich Rosenstiehl, 1st sergeant of Captain Wietersheim's Grenadier Company, died 3 November in the barracks at Quebec. Born in Holtzhalleben, in Schwarzburg-Sondershausen, he was of the Evangelical faith, and a tailor by trade. He left a wife, without children behind, and was 28 years old.

67. Christoph Bomberg, private in Captain Gogel's Company, died 4 November in the hospital Hotel de Dieu, at Quebec. Born in Gotha, he was of the Evangelical faith, and was 36 years old.

68. Friederich Harms, private in Captain Prince of Schwarzburg's Company, died 5 November in the hospital Hotel de Dieu, at Quebec. Born in Jever, he was of the Evangelical faith, and a linen-weaver by trade. He left a wife with two sons and two daughters behind. He was 48 years old.

69. Johann Adams, was murdered at his post on the ship wharf, at Quebec, on the night of 5 November, and thrown into the St. Lawrence River. His murderers have never been caught, although some sailors were arrested. From all indications, it must

have been sailors, because his post had the task of preventing sailors from going to, or coming from the ships after ten o'clock at night, which had been a daily source of friction. His head wound was apparently the result of being hit with a bottle, as glass was found in his skull. He was a member of Major von Rauschenplat's Company. Born in Copenhagen, he was of the Evangelical faith, and 21 years old.

70. Wilhelm Hesse, private in Major von Rauschenplat's Company, died 6 November in the hospital Hotel de Dieu, in Quebec. Born in Wollgramshausen, in Schwarzburg, he was 19 years old.

71. Heinrich Hundstock, of Captain Piquet's Grenadier Company, died 14 November, in the hospital Hotel de Dieu, at Quebec. Born in Zerbst, he was of the Evangelical faith, and was 18 years old.

72. Daniel Schmidt, jaeger private in the Anhalt-Zerbst Jaeger Corps, died 15 [November], in the hospital Hotel de Dieu, in Quebec. He was born in Zerbst, of the Evangelical faith, and left a son and daughter behind. He was 24 years old.

73. Joseph Kayser, private in Major von Rauschenplat's Company, died 21 November in the hospital Hotel de Dieu, at Quebec. Born in Switzerland, of the Catholic faith, he was a tailor by

trade. He was married, and 23 years old.

74. Georg Wipling, private in Major von Rauschenplat's Company, died 21 November, in the hospital Hotel de Dieu, at Quebec. Born in Jever, he was of the Evangelical faith, and a tailor by trade. He left a wife behind, and was 37 years old.

75. Hajo Eden Onken, a member of Captain Piquet's Grenadier Company, died 22 November in the hospital Hotel de Dieu, at Quebec. Born in Wittmund, of the Evangelical faith, he was a basket-maker by trade. He was married, and 36 years old.

76i Carl Ludewich Christian Haberlandt;. The only son of Private Gottfried Haberlandt, of Major von Rauschenplat's Company, died 23 November, in the barracks, at Quebec. He was 3 days old.

77. Johann Andreas Matthaes, private in Major von Rauschenplat's Company, died 23 November, in the hospital Hotel de Dieu, at Quebec. Born at Schluesselfeld, in Wuerburg, he was of the Catholic faith. He was 28 years old.

78. Viet Henkelmann, died 23 November, in the hospital Hotel de Dieu, at Quebec. He was a private in Major von Rauschenplat's Company, Born in Schluesselfeld, in Wuerzburg, of the Catholic faith, and 28 years old.

79. Peter Fresdorff, private in Captain Gogel's Company, died 29 November, in the hospital Hotel de Dieu, at Quebec. Born in the Zerbst suburb named Ankuhn, he was of the Evangelical faith. He was 31 years old.

80. Jacob Gruber, private in Colonel von Rauschenplat's Company, died 4 December, in the hospital Hotel de Dieu, at Quebec. Born at Neustadt, in Bavaria, he was of the Catholic faith, and 19 years old.

81. Christoph Fischer, private in Colonel von Rauschenplat's Company, died 7 December, in the hospital Hotel de Dieu, at Quebec. Born at Seberode, he was of the Evangelical faith, and 25 years old.

82. Joseph Springer, private in Major von Rauschenplat's Company, died 10 December, in the hospital Hotel de Dieu, at Quebec. Born in Prague, he was of the Catholic faith, and a cloth-maker by trade. He was 22 years old.

83. Christoph Timme, private in Captain Gogel's Company, died 11 December in the hospital Hotel de Dieu, at Quebec. Born Verden, he was of the Evangelical faith, and 57 years old. He was married, and left a son and daughter behind in Jever.

84. Reinhardt Ihnen, private in Colonel von Rauchenplat's Company, died 19 December, in the

hospital Hotel de Dieu, in Quebec. Born in Jever, he was of the Evangelical faith, and 34 years old. He left a wife, a son, and two daughters behind.

85. Peter Fischer, private in Captain Piquet's Grenadier Company, died on 19 December, in the hospital Hotel de Dieu, at Quebec. Born in Jever, he was of the Evangelical faith, and 25 years old.

86. Christoph Ostermann, private in Captain Piquet's Grenadier Company, died 20 December in the hospital Hotel de Dieu, at Quebec. Born at Ganglofsoemmern, in Saxony, he was of the Evangelical faith, and a mason by trade. He left a wife, two sons, and two daughters behind. He was 44 years old.

    Total of dead since 27 February 1778,
    the day of the departure from Zerbst
    86 Persons
    71 Men
    6 Women
    9 Children, 5 sons, and 4 daughters

Of which, there died aboard ship on the sea voyage:
    17 Men
    2 Women
    2 Children

Note: Of the above number, 2 were unnatural deaths, numbers 31 and 69.

Death Register for the Year 1779

87. Gottlob Fischer, private in Major von Rauschenplat's Company, died 7 January, in the hospital Hotel de Dieu, at Quebec. Born at Hirschberg, in Silesia. He was of the Evangelical faith, and had learned commerce. He was 33 years old.

88. Heinrich Fister, private in Captain Prince of Schwarzburg's Company, died 10 January in the hospital Hotel de Dieu, at Quebec. Born at Otterstadt, in Schwarzburg, he was of the Evangelical faith, and a linen-weaver by trade. He was 34 years old.

89. Friederich Bonnius, private in Captain Piquet's Grenadier Company, died 12 January in the hospital Hotel de Dieu, at Quebec. Born in Oldenburg, he was of the Evangelical faith, and 26 years old.

90. Johann Frerichs, private in Captain von Wietersheim's Grenadier Company, died 22 January, in the hospital Hotel de Dieu, at Quebec. Born in Jever, of the Evangelical faith, he was a shoemaker by trade, and 23 years old.

91. Heinrich Vasse, private in Captain Prince of Schwarzburg's Company, died 5 February in the hospital Hotel de Dieu, at Quebec. Born at Klingen, in Schwarzburg, he was of the Evangelical faith, and 18 years old.

92. Friederich Leitheiser, private in the company of the brigade-major, Captain Piquet, died 7 February, in the hospital Hotel de Dieu, at Quebec. Born in Altona, he was of the Evangelical faith, and a baker by trade. He was 23 years old.

93. Caspar Hartung, private in the company of the Brigadier General, Colonel von Rauschenplat, died 8 February, in the hospital Hotel de Dieu. Born at Muehlhausen, he was of the Evangelical faith, and 24 years old.

94. Joseph Friedmann, private in the brigade-major, Captain Piquet's Grenadier Company, died 24 February, in the hospital Hotel de Dieu, at Quebec. Born at Maschau, in German Bohemia, he was of the Catholic faith, and a tanner by trade. He was 24 years old.

95. Friederich Reinhardt, jaeger private in the Anhalt-Zerbsdt Jaeger Corps, died 1 March in the hospital Hotel de Dieu, at Quebec. Born at Ratenau, in Prussia, he was of the Evangelical faith, and a linen-weaver by trade. He was 21 years old.

96. Gottfried Larosch, private in Brigade-major, Captain Piquet's Grenadier Company, died 2 March in the hospital Hotel de Dieu, at Quebec. Born in Zerbst, and of the Evangelical faith, he was a shoemaker by trade, and 35 years old.

97. Andreas Hillbergt, private in Captain von Wietersheim's Grenadier Company, died 10 March in the hospital Hotel de Dieu, at Quebec. Born at Kuhberge, in Anhalt-Zerbst, he was of the Evangelical faith, and 34 years old.

98. Wilhelm Jantzen, private in Captain Gogel's Company, died 11 March, in the hospital Hotel de Dieu, at Quebec. Born in Jever, of the Evangelical faith. He was married, and left his wife, a son, and two daughters behind. He was 51 years old.

99. Anthon Micholau, jaeger private in the Anhalt-Zerbst Jaeger Corps, died at sea, 16 May, aboard the recruit transport from Germany. Born in Philippsburg, and of the Catholic faith, he had learned commerce. He was 18 years old.

100. Christian Kiesel, captain-at-arms in Captain von Wietersheim's Grenadieer Company, died 31 May in the barracks at Quebec. Born in Zerbst, and of the Evangelical faith, he was a mason by trade. He was married, and left his wife and a daughter behind in Roslau, in Anhalt-Zerbst. He was 29 years old.

101. Christoph Auerbach, private in Captain Prince of Schwarzburg's Company, died on 23 June, in the barracks, at Quebec. Born in Chemnitz, in Saxony, he was of the Evangelical faith, and a miller by trade. He was 26 years old.

102. Michael Vollrath, drowned on the afternoon of 4 July, after saying that he was going to bathe in the St. Charles River, near Quebec. It is not clear whether he drowned with intent, or by accident, but the first seems the case, as the river in the area where he was found is not deep enough for someone to easily drown therein. He was buried without ceremony by the regiment, in the English cemetery. He was a member of Captain Gogel's Company, of the Evangelical faith, and a linen-weaver by trade. Born in Rodleben, in Scwarzburg, he was 24 years old.

103. Gottfried Wagener, of Captain Gogel's Company, hanged himself on the grounds of the barracks, at Quebec, on 5 July. Born at Potsdam, he was of the Evangelical faith, and a rope-maker by trade. He was 22 years old. He was buried quietly outside the churchyard, by the regimental servants.

104. Christian Goericke, private in Captain von Wietersheim's Grenadier Company, died 14 August, in the sick room of the barracks, at Quebec. Born in the village of Fletz, in Anhalt-Zerbst, he was of the Evangelical faith, and was 21 years old.

105. Andrea Bauer, private of Captain Prince of Schwarzburg's Company, died 15 August, in Charlebourg Parish, a city lying near Quebec, while on a work command, and was buried at that place. Born

at Freistadt, in Silesia, he was of the Evangelical faith, and a hat maker by trade. He was 29 years old.

106. Christian Grashoff, of the Brigadier-general, Colonel von Rauschenplat's Company, died 9 October, while working on the defenses near Quebec. He was suddenly struck by a stone during the blasting, in which he was engaged, and killed. He was buried in the English cemetery, with full military honors. Born at Quedlinburg, he was of the Evangelical faith, and 19 years old.

107. Oldmann Frerics, died aboard ship, on the St. Lawrence River, on 5 October, and was buried on land. The ship was carrying the first recruit transport from Germany. He was born at Sillenstaedt, in Jever, of the Evangelical faith, and was 20 years old.

108a. Sophia Maria Catherina Schroeckin, the small daughter of Private Schroeck, of Captain Prince of Schwarzburg's Company, died 21 October, in the barracks, at Quebec. She was 3 weeks old.

109b. Johann Peter Krug, the first born son of Private Krug, of Captain Gogel's Company, died 3 November, in the barracks, at Quebec. He was 1 month and 1 week old.

110. Friederich Stangen, private of Captain von Wietersheim's Grenadier Company, died 17 November, in the hospital Hotel de Dieu, at Quebec.

Born at Immenrode, in Schwarzburg-Rudelstaedt, he was of the Evangelical faith, and 32 years old. He had left his wife behind in Stade, in Electoral Hannover.
     Total Deaths in the Year 1779
       24 Persons
       22 Men and
        2 Children, 1 son, 1 daughter
Note: Among those deaths, 3 died of unnatural causes.

Death Register for the Year 1780

111. Johann Lein, a member of Captain Prince of Schwarzburg's Company, froze to death during the night of 23 January, in the Parish of St. Francois, in the District of Quebec. He had been at the canteen, had something to drink, but according to his comrades, was not drunk. During suddenly occurring bad weather, he could not find his house and froze to death on the street. Born in the village of Wetzhausen, in Greater Darmstadt, he was of the Evangelical faith, and a tailor by trade. He was 28 years old.

112. Heinrich Albers, of Captain von Wietersheim's Grenadier Company, died 26 January, in the Parish of St. Thomas South, in the District of Quebec. Born at Niende, in Jever, he was of the Evangelical faith, and 26 years old. He left a wife, without children, behind in Jever.

113. Friederich Wendt, committed suicide with his own weapon, in the garden of his host, in the Parish of St. Pierre, in the District of Quebec, on 17 February. He had previously attempted suicide in the garden, but been prevented from doing so. For that, he had been punished with a demotion, which caused him severe depression, and made him very sick. He was given his former rank, and restored to duty, and conducted himself in a proper manner, except at times, he

complained about his sorry fate, because he had been a student in the orphans' home in Halle. He wished to spend his time studying, but was prevented from doing so. His depression returned suddenly, while in the country, so that he silently loaded his weapon, and upon leaving the room of his host, said that he was going bird-shooting, but then shot himself, in the garden. He was a corporal in Captain Gogel's Company, born at Erlangen, in Bayreuth. He was 25 years old.

114x. Christoph Heyderichs' wife delivered a still-born daughter on 3 March, in the Parish of St. Pierre, in the District of Quebec.

115. Christoph Lindauer, drowned on 30 April, in the South River, in the Parish of St. Thomas, in the District of Quebec. This parish is divided lengthwise by the said river, and settled on both sides, so that one-half of the people, each time, when they wish to go to church, must cross the river. Such was the case for this unfortunate individual. He wished to cross the river, to where his quarters lay, but the river was swollen by the heavy thawing, and by nature, was exceptionally rapid. The wind was extra strong, and the soldiers were afraid, but because the inhabitants, who knew the nature of the river best, traveled with them, they entered the canoe (a rather frightful vessel

cut from a tree, and, if one can picture it, very much like a trough). When they reached the middle of the river, which was about 500 yards wide, the raging current tipped the canoe over, and all the occupants were thrown into the water. Two farmers and two soldiers saved themselves, but this unfortunate individual, and one of the local residents, gave up their lives. He was a member of Brigade-major, Captain Piquet's Grenadier Company, born in Erfurth. He was of the Catholic faith, married, and had left his wife behind in Jever. He was buried in a festive military style, in the parish cemetery, at the specific written request of one of the Catholic inhabitants of the parish, by the name of Methonbash, to the commander, because Lindauer was of the Catholic faith.

Note: I should note here that as long as we were in this land, not even while in the barracks, no one, not of the Catholic religion, could be buried in a cemetery, as the inhabitants were too scrupulous to allow that. Therefore, a satisfactory place had to be located each time, where the body could be interned. Usually, the selected spot was where a crucifix had been erected, and where, in most cases, an encircling fence had been placed. Although this was not allowed, either, as we never asked, there was never a complaint, and no refusal.

116. Peter Schottler, member of Captain Gogel's Company, died 19 May, in the Parish of St. Pierre, in the District of Quebec. Born in Guntheim, in the Pfalz, he was of the Catholic faith, and 18 years old.

117. Maria Elisabeth Piquet, the only daughter of the Brigade-major, Captain Piquet, died 19 June, at Quebec. She was 10 days old.

118, Christiana Elisabeth Paulin, [infant daughter], of Private Paul, of Captain von Wietersheim's Grenadier Company, died 24 June, at Quebec. She was 1 month and 1 week old.

119. Ferdinand Fritz, a member of Major von Rauschenplat's Company, drowned in the South River, in St. Thomas, on 25 June. He was drunk, and waded several times through the mentioned river, where it was shallow, and each time crossed successfully. Despite the frequent warning of his comrades, he continued to do so until he missed the shallow portion, fell in a hole, which had a whirlpool, of which there were many in this river, was torn from the firm footing, and drowned therein, without hope of rescue. After several days, his body was found some miles down stream, at St. Pierre, and quietly buried. Born at Adelberg, in Wuerttenberg, he was of the Evangelical faith, and a miller by trade. He was 26 years old.

HESSIAN CHAPLAINS

120. Christoph Johann, private in Brigade-major, Captain Piquet's Grenadier Company, died 20 July, in the Parish of St. Thomas. Born in the Grafschaft of Laisch, he was of the Catholic faith, a butcher by trade, and 21 years old.

121d. Christiana Catharina Kreyselerin, the small daughter of Private Kreyseler, carpenter in Captain von Wietersheim's Grenadier Company, died 26 August, in the Parish of Beauport, in the District of Quebec. She was 1 month and 3 days old.

122. Friederich Krause, after ten o'clock in the evening, of 5 September, shot himself with the rifle of Captain Runkel, whose servant he was, in Runkel's tent, in the camp at Pointe Levi. At that time, he had an attack of melancholy, because when he had been the servant of a man in Paris, that man had been stabbed to death, for which Krause was partially responsible. After the tent was taken down, he was buried the same night, by the regimental servants, at the spot where he had shot himself. Born in Breslau, he was of the Evangelical faith, and 28 years old.

123. Christian Dront, a member of the senior sergeant-major [Oberwachtmeister] von Rauschenplat's Company, died 13 September, in the hospital Hotel de Dieu, at Quebec. Born in Brunigwald, in Saarbruecken, he was of the Evangelical faith, and 25

years old.

124. Heinrich Kloesneck, a member of Major von Rauschenplat's Company, died 18 September, in the camp at Pointe Levi. Born at Tiefenthal, in Erfurt, he was of the Evangelical faith, and 29 years old.

125. Christoph Hinderichs, carpenter in Brigademajor, Captain Piquet's Grenadier Company, died 14 November, in the Parish of Becancour. Born at Oehen, in East Friesland, he was of the Evangelical faith, a carpenter by trade, and 33 years old.

Recapitualtion
Of the Deaths for the Year 1780
11 Men, of whom 5 deaths were unnatural
(see 111, 113, 115, 119, and 122)
4 Children, 3 daughters, and 1 son
15 Total

Death Register
For the Year 1781

126. Jacob Berger, a member of Captain Prince of Schwarzburg's Company, died 18 February, in the hospital of St. Antoine Parish, and was buried there. Born at Coswig, in Anhalt-Zerbst, he was of the Evangelical faith, and 22 years old.

127. Johann August Heyne, servant of Chaplain Braunsdorf, hanged himself in the chaplain's quarters, in Becancour Parish. He became melancholy, during a three week absence of his master, and while in this mood, hanged himself. He was a member of the Brigade-major, Captain Piquet's Grenadier Company, born in Zerbst, of the Evangelical faith, and 22 years old.

128. Johann Schulmeyer, private in Major von Rauschenplat's Company, died 28 February, in the Becancour Parish hospital, in the District of Trois Rivieres. Born in Potsdam, he was of the Evangelical faith, a tailor by trade, and 19 years old.

129. Christian Hoffmann, committed suicide by shooting himself, with his own weapon, in the living room of his quarters, in Becancour Parish, in the District of Trois Rivieres, on 17 April. The reason, as he was never melancholy, may never be determined. He was a corporal in Brigade-major, Captain Piquet's

Grenadier Company. Born Eulenburg, in Saxony, he was of the Evangelical faith, a shoemaker by trade, and 26 years old. He was buried the same day, by the regimental servants.

130. Johann Janssen, private in Captain von Wietersheim's Grenadier Company, died 20 April, in the hospital Hotel de Dieu, at Quebec. Born in Oldenburg, he was of the Evangelical faith, and 45 years old. He left a wife and two daughters behind in Jever.

131. Christian Thiele, drowned in an unknown and unfortunate manner, in the Gentilly River, in Gentilly Parish, in the District of Trois Rivieres. A jaeger private in the Anhalt-Zerbst Jaeger Corps, he was born in Koenigslutter, in Brunswick, of the Evangelical faith, a tanner by trade, and 26 years old.

132a. Anthon Ludewig, the small son of the Carpenter Ludewig, of Captain Gogel's Company, died in an unfortunate, and unexpected manner, on 15 May. The child fell into a kettle of boiling water, and although pulled out immediately, it was too late, and he gave up the ghost. He was buried in Nicolet Parish, where the accident occurred. He was 1 year, 9 months, and 2 weeks old.

133b. Anna Sophia Magdalena Barthsen, the small daughter of Private Barth, of Captain Prince of

Schwarzburg's Company, died 9 July, in the Parish of La Bay St. Antoine. She was 1 year, 9 months, 3 weeks, and 5 days old.

134s. Dorothea Sophia Mastin, the young daughter of Private Paul Mast, of Captain von Wietersheim's Grenadier Company, died 14 August, in the barracks at Quebec. She was 3 years, 7 months, 1 week, and 4 days old.

135. Georg Nohre, Private in Brigade-major, Captain Piquet's Grenadier Company, died 20 August, in the service of the King, in an unfortunate manner, while cutting wood, in St. Jean Parish, in the District of Montreal. While cutting down trees, one fell on him, and he was buried there. Born at Sondershausen, in Schwarzburg, he was of the Evangelical faith, a miller by trade, and 31 years old.

136. Johann Heinrich Hass, Private in Brigade-major, Captain Piquet's Grenadier Company, died 3 September, in the hospital Hotel de Dieu, in Quebec. Born in Jever, of the Evangelical faith, and a miller by trade, he was 42 years old.

137. Philipp Kalb committed suicide on 19 September, in the quarters of Lieutenant von Heringen, in Becancour Parish, in the District of Trois Rivieres. He shot himself with a small hunting rifle, during the absence of his master, the lieutenant, and

was buried there by the regimental servants. Born at Tylle, in Schwarzburg, he was of the Evangelical faith, a saltpeter refiner by trade, and 26 years old.

138. Heinrich Matern, drowned in the Becancour River, in Becancour Parish, in the District of Trois Rivieres, on 9 October, while transporting the royal provisions. The boat was heavily laden, and the wind was very strong. The boat capsized in the middle of the river. The other occupants were able to save themselves, but Matern, who was an excellent swimmer, and could handle this type of vessel very well, drowned. His body was found nine days later, and he was buried with full military honors. He was a corporal in Brigade-major, Captain Piquet's Grenadier Company, born at Speyer, and 26 years old. He was of the Evangelical faith, and a baker by trade.

139. Carl Friederich Meyne, died in an unknown manner, on 28 October, in St. Pierre Parish, in the District of Trois Rivieres. On that day, he had been with Captain von Wietersheim, at that place, and planned to return to his quarters at Becancour. There were many deep valleys lying between, and he apparently fell down one of the hillsides, because he was fond of drinking, rolled into the St. Lawrence River and drowned, because it was reported that his body was found in the river at Quebec. He was the

regimental assistant surgeon, born in Schoennebeck, of the Evangelical faith, and his age was unknown.

140. Georg Christian Harms, drowned in the St. Lawrence River, on 3 November, while the regiment was moving into winter quarters. He was traveling with the baggage, on the water, when a storm arose, which caused the boat to start to pitch. When this happened, because he was sitting on a case, he was thrown from the batteau, a rather large vessel, similar to a sloop, and fell into the water. Because there were numerous vessels of this type traveling close together, it was impossible to rescue him, and unfortunately, he drowned. He was a regimental assistant surgeon, born at Hamburg, of the Evangelical faith, and 22 years old.

141. Adam Apfel, died 28 November in the St. Croix Parish hospital , in the District of Quebec, after running the gauntlet. As a corporal, he had led a group of privates into stealing. Once, they had broken into a merchant's business at night, and stolen bolts of all sorts of silk, cotton, and linen, as much as they could carry, which was first discovered after nearly half a year, as a result of the theft of a small amount of sugar. As the gang leader, because he, at the same time, had misled his comrades, he was sentenced to hang, which sentence was then reduced to running a gauntlet of 200 men, 36 times, on three successive

days, twelve times each day. This was carried out, and as a result, he gave up the ghost, three days later. After being demoted, he was a member of Captain Gogel's Company. Born at Muehlhausen, he was of the Evangelical faith, a cooper by trade, and 24 years old.

    Total Deaths during the Year 1781
     16 Persons
     13 Men
      3 Children, 1 son, who died
       accidentally, and 2 daughters

 Among the 13 men who died, 9 were from unnatural causes.

Death Register
For the Year 1782

142. Andreas Herrmann, a member of Captain Prince of Schwarzburg's Company, died 20 April, in St. Croix Parish, in the District of Quebec. Born in Kluecken, in Anhalt-Zerbst, he was of the Evangelical faith, and 22 years old.

143. Heer Oncken, of Brigade-major, Captain Piquet's Grenadier Company, died 22 May, in the St. Croix Parish hospital, in the District of Quebec. Born in Jever, of the Evangelical faith, and 29 years old.

NB: [Herrmann] died on this date in the year 1783.

144. Christoph Hartmann, a member of Captain Gogel's Company, died 23 June, in the St. Croix Parish hospital, in the District of Quebec. Born at Thiele, in Schwarzburg, he was of the Evangelical faith, and 30 years old.

145. Christiana Margaretha Jacobin, wife of Captain-at-arms Jacobi, of Lieutenant Colonel von Rauschenplat's Company, died 24 July, in the camp at Pointe Levi, near Quebec. She was born in Wolmerstaedt, near Magdeburg, daughter of a citizen and wheel-maker by the name of Schaefer. She was of the Evangelical faith, and 56 years old.

146. Christian Schmidt, corporal in Captain Gogel's Company, died 29 August in the hospital Hotel de Dieu, at Quebec. Born in Zerbst, he was married, and had left his wife behind. Of the Evangelical faith, and a rope-maker by trade, he was 30 years old.

147. Catharina Eleanore Carolina Schroeckin, the small daughter of Private Schroeck, of Captain Prince of Schwarzburg's Company, died 4 September, in the barracks at Pointe Levi, near Quebec. She was 1 year, 8 months, and 6 days old.

148. Jacob Matthaes, private in Captain Prince of Schwarzburg's Company, died 8 September, in the camp hospital at Pointe Levi, near Quebec. Born at Burgweiler, in the Reich, he was of the Catholic faith, and 26 years old.

Total Deaths
During the Year 1782
7 Persons
5 Men
1 Woman, and
1 Child

Death Register
For the Year 1783

149. Andreas Reuter, of Lieutenant Colonel von Rauschenplat's Company, died 2 February, in the River Quelle Parish hospital, in the District of Quebec, born Chemnitz, in Saxony, he was of the Evangelical faith, a linen-weaver by trade, and 25 years old.

150. Anna Catharina Sophia Schmidtin, infant daughter of Private Schmidt, of Lieutenant Colonel von Rauschenplat's Company, died 23 February, in River Quelle Parish, in the District of Quebec. She was 7 days old.

151. Heinrich Harms, froze to death on 4 March, in St. Roi Parish, in the District of Quebec. He was drunk, and in the evening was returning to his quarters, which sat high on a cliff. He apparently injured himself in a fall, and lay unconscious until he froze to death, A private in Captain Nuppenau's Company, born in Hoelldorff, in East Friesland, he was of the Evangelical faith, and 28 years old.

152. Heinrich Schiede, froze to death on 12 March, in River Quelle Parish, in the District of Quebec. From all indications, he chose this death himself, because he had wandered into a field in which a haystack stood, stripped off his winter clothing, sat down on the haystack, and awaited his

death. He was a private in Brigade-major, Captain Piquet's Grenadier Company. Born in Lauterbach, in Hesse-Darmstadt, he was of the Reformed faith, and 35 years old.

154. August Nuppenau, Only son of Captain Nuppenau, died 20 April, in St. Roi Parish, in the District of Quebec. He was 6 months old.

Note: Heer Oncken died on 22 May . (see #143)

155. Matthias Michaleck, died in the woods, in St. Anne Parish, in the lower District of Quebec, on 3 June. It is not possible to determine whether or not he chose this manner of death. Previously, he had committed numerous excesses, for which he was demoted from corporal to private. This had made him very melancholy, and later, he and several comrades, beat up a farmer, resulting in his having to run the gauntlet. On the same day that he returned to the company from the hospital, he put some bread in his bread sack, and walked for more than an hour into the woods, to where no one was to be expected. However, a farmer out hunting, came across the body lying by a tree. The head had been beaten, or hit against a tree, until it bled. He was a private in Brigade-major, Captain Piquet's Grenadier Company. Born in

Steckenau, in Bohemia, he had been a Catholic, but converted to the Lutheran faith in Zerbst. He had trained as a hunter, and was 28 years old.

156. Johann Hoffmann, died 12 September, on board the English transport ship *Ann*, on the trip from America to Germany, and was buried in the sea, in the channel between England and France, the same day. He was a member of Lieutenant Colonel von Rauschenplat's Company, born in Rabitzka, in Poland, of the Evangelical faith, and 40 years old.

157. Johann Luding, drowned at Hocksiel, in the Hocksiel Deep, in an unfortunate manner, on 29 September. The ships on which the regiment had arrived there, were lying so close together, that it was possible to jump from one to the other. He tried to do this, but the ships parted, and he fell into the gap between the ships, where, although he was immediately pulled up, he died. He was buried at the Hocksiel, also. A member of Captain Prince of Scchwarzburg's Company, he had been born in Hameln, in Hannover. He was of the Evangelical faith, a tailor by trade, and 32 years old.

158. Wilhelm Mueller, of Captain Prince of Schwarzburg's Company, died 22 October, at Jever, and was buried there on the 24th. A member of Captain Prince of Schwarzburg's Company, and of the

Evangelical faith, he was 40 years old.

159. Johann Wegesser, corporal in Brigadier von Rauschenplat's Company, died 22 November in Jever, and was buried there the same day. Born at Wechtersbach, in Isenburg, he was of the Reformed faith, and 22 years old.

Total Deaths

During the Year 1783

10 Men, of whom 4 were unnatural deaths

2 Children, one son, and one daughter

12 Total

- - - - - - -

Death Register

For the Year 1784

160. Johanna Sophia Margaretha Ehnen, infant daughter of Private Ehnen, of Captain Nuppenau's Company, died 28 April, in the barracks at Jever. She was 3 weeks and 4 days old.

161. Abraham Paul, of Brigade-major, Captain Picquet's Grenadier Company, died 5 July, at the hospital at Jever. Born at Oppenhein, in Electoral Pfalz, he was of the Evangelical faith, and 24 years old.

- - - - - - -

Death Register
For the Year 1785

162. Johann Christian Friederich Roehrs, infant son of Private Roehrs, of Captain Prince of Schwarzburg's Company, died 27 January, in the barracks at Jever. He was 9 days old.

163. Franz Heyd, private in Brigade-major, Captain Piquet's Grenadier Company, died 2 February, in the barracks at Jever, and was buried there on the 4th, with full military honors. Born in Fulda, and of the Catholic faith, he served the company as oboist. He was 33 years old, and left a wife and child behind.

164. Johann August Wipling, infant son of the widow Wipling, died 6 March, at the age of 2 months.

165. David Friederich Ehnen, young son of Private Ehnen, of Captain Nuppenau's Company, died in the barracks at Jever, on 11 April. He was 5 years, and 6 months old.

HESSIAN CHAPLAINS

Church Book Kept for the Troops of the Ruler of Anhalt-Zerbst in the Service of the King of England
(Part 2)

Although it was mentioned in Part 1 of this article, that only the death listing of the Anhalt-Zerbst Church Book was available, Michael P. Palmer, of the German Genealogical Society of America provided a copy of the Norddeutsche Familienkunde *for January-March 1986, in which Brigitte Heinicke and Georg Jahn published the remaining portions of the Church Book maintained by Chaplain Braunsdorf, and currently in the church archives at Jever, Germany.*

The following is my translation of a portion of Heinicke and Hahn's article on the Anhalt-Zerbst Church Book, and some of their introductory remarks.. The church book covers births/baptisms and marriages. Their work was published in alphabetical order, but in my translation I have used the same sequence as used by Chaplain Johann Gottlieb Siegismund Braunsdorf. When two dates are listed in the birth/baptism, it is assumed that the first is the birthday, and the second the date of the baptism. The term private baptism has been used when baptism was administered under emergency conditions, fearing an early death. Those infants whose names are followed by an asterisk, are also listed in the death lists of the church book, which follows this article. It will be seen that Braunsdorf served other German and English units, as well as those of Anhalt-Zerbst. Finally, a letter e has been used after vowels a, o, and u to indicate an umlaut, in the German text.

- - - - - - - -

An Anhalt Military Church Book in Jever
By Brigittee Heinicke and Georg Jahn
Translated and transcribed by Bruce E..Burgoyne

- - - - - - -

The Evangelical-Lutheran Church Archives at Jever/Ostfriesland maintain a very well preserved church book, in folio format, which has the title: *Kirchenbuch gefuehrt ueber Sr. Hochfuerstlichen Durchlaucht zu Anhalt-Zerbst, in Koeniglich Grossbrittanischen Sold stehenden Truppen enthaltend das Todten, Tauf, und Trau Register angefangen den 21sten Febr. 1778 als dem Tage des Abmarsches aus Zerbst von M. Johann Gottlieb Siegismund Braunsdorf Feldprediger,* or, in English, Church Book maintained on the troops of His Serene Highness of Anhalt-Zerbst in the service of the King of Great Britain, containing the deaths, baptisms, and marriage register, beginning on 21 February 1778, the day of marching from Zerbst by M. Johann Gottlieb Siegismund Braunsdorf, Chaplain.

The compiler, Johann Gottlieb Siegismund Braunsdorf (31 March 1752-1826), holder of a master's degree, was a native of Zerbst, whose father was a ticking and damask weaver. He studied from 1773 to 1775 in Wittensberg, and in 1776 in Halle. Thereafter he was employed as the private tutor of the Rauschenplat family in Zerbst. It is not clear by which of the two (half)-brothers [he was employed], Christian Friedrich Johann Ludolf August Rauschenplat (1730-1799), a brigadier general in Zerbst in 1784; or Johann Georg Heinrich Rauschenplat (1742-1810), the Anhalt-Dessau colonel and commandant of the city of Zerbst. Braunsdorf became the field chaplain of the troops which the Prince of Anhalt-Zerbst sold to King George III of England in 1777, and which were commanded by the older of the Rauschenplat brothers. Braunsdorf gave both Rauschenplats the title of count, although neither was such. At the end of the deployment in North America and the return to Germany in the fall of 1784, Braunsdorf remained in Jever (The domain of Jever belonged to the Principality of Anhalt-Zerbst from 1667 to 1793.), and continued to serve the troops in the garrison in Jever, at least in part, as he also sought a parish in that place. In 1784 he married a Miss Chemnitz of Jever, and became the pastor at Waddewarden, near Jever, on 24 June 1785. His entries in the Anhalt Church Book end suddenly in May 1785. Braunsdorf died after more than 40 years of activity. The exact date of his death in 1826 is unknown.

Supplemental Information

During the publication process, the authors accidentally obtained interesting supplemental material from Herr [Mr.] Wolfgang Buesing of Olenburg, which with his generosity is included here. (The article "Die Familie Chemnitz", in the *Oldenburg Burgischen Hauskalender,* 1986.) From the chronicle of the Chemnitz family, now in a private collection, which were maintained since 1793 by Pastor Johann Ludwig Chemnitz (1750-1822), a member of the Consistorial Court at Jever, the following is quoted:

"Christina Wilhelmina Chemnitz, born after 1750 in Zerbst, the daughter of Christian Gottfried Chemnitz, who held a master's degree and was an assistant judge of the Consistorial Court and pastor at Zerbst, and his second wife, Sophie Wilhelmina Restel, married on 10 August 1784 in Zerbst, Johann Gottlieb Siergismund Braunsdorf, the compiler of the Anhalt Church Book. A son, Franz Siegismund

Wilhelm, was born to the couple on 31 May 1785 in Waddewarden. The mother died two weeks later, on 15 August 1785. The younger Braunsdorf was engaged as the second pastor at Waddewarden in 1814 - his father was the first pastor there - but died when only 33 years old, on 29 April 1818. He was survived by a daughter, Johanna (Hannchen) whose further fate and eventual descendants are unknown."

The quoted chronicle also gives the exact date of [the elder] Braunsdorf as 2 November 1825. Therefore, he outlived his son by seven years. The compiler to the chronicle was the older brother of Christina W. Chemnitz, married to Braunsdorf.

MARRIAGES

1. Koch, Andreas - Corporal, Green Grenadier Company, from Anhalt-Zerbst, married Sophia Schmidt, from Zerbst, on 21 February 1778, on the march at the first night's quarters at Roslau.

2. Heyderich, Christopher - Private, Rauschenplat's Company, from Berghel, married Dorothea Maria Nohr, from Sondershausen, on 27 February 1778, on the march at Boherna (?), in Saxony.

3. Haberland, Gottfried - Private, Rauschenplat's Company, from Zerbst, married Johannna Elizabeth Briening, from Loburg (?), in Magdeburg, on 27 February 1778, on the march at Boherna (?), in Saxony.

4. Barths, Johann Friedrich - Private, Schwarzburg's Company, from Magdeburg, married Maria Dorothea Kellain, from Kreussen, in Schwarzburg, on 8 March 1778, on the march at Grossen Bruechter (?), near Sondershausen.

5. Ludewig, Anthon - Carpenter, Green Grenadier Company, married Anna Magdalena Nohr, from Sondershausen (sister of the bride in #2?), on 8 March 1778 at Klein-Bruechter, in Schwarzburg.

6. Ramhorst, Friedrich - Private, Piquet's Company, married Catherina Margaretha Trauche, daughter of the Hannover Cavalry Sergeant-major

HESSIAN CHAPLAINS

Trauche, on 9 April 1778 at Stade.

7. Steineck, Johann Georg Christoph - Private, Piquet's Company, from Frankenhausen, married Anna Catherina Crass (or Cross?), widow, on 4 June 1778, on the transport ship *Sally* in the English harbor at Torbay.

8. Schenk, Bernhard - Sergeant-major, Piquet's Company, from Jever, (brother of #28?), married the widow Christina Sophia Rosenstiel, on 30 December 1778, in the barracks at Quebec.

9. Ruff, Michael - Private, Rauschenplat's Company, from Petersen, in the Palatinate (?), married the widow, Juliana Dorothea Preiss, (Catholic), on 20 April 1779, in the barracks at Quebec, after receiving special permission.

10. Piquet, (Carl Friedrich) - Grenadier Captain, from Muempelgard, in Switzerland, was married to a [Miss] Skeene, daughter of the English Colonel Skeene, by the English Chaplain Montmolin, on 26 April 1779, at Quebec.

11. Nuppenau, Johann August Zacharias - Captain-lieutenant, from Zerbst, married Marie Riverin (Catholic), daughter of the deceased merchant Riverin from Quebec, on 12 December 1780, at Mon Loretto/Quebec.

HESSIAN CHAPLAINS

12. Hoffmann, Johann Albrecht - of the Jaeger Corps, from Langendorf, in Weissenfeld, married Marie Therese Bilanger, from St. Thomas/Quebec (Catholic), on 2 December 1781, at St. Antoine/Quebec.

13. Bretker, Johann Christian - Private, Schwarzburg's Company, from Terbuhr (?), in Anhalt-Coethen, married Marie Magdalene Grammond (Catholic), from LaBaye, St.Antoine/Trois Rivieres, on 12 December 1781 at St. Antoine/Quebec.

14. Winter, Martin - Private, Rauschenplat's Company, from Wisbaden [Wiesbaden?], married the widow, Sophia Buhlmann, from Stade, on 4 January 1783, at Riviere Quelle/Quebec.

15. Koenig, Johann Heinrich - Private, Wietersheim's Company, from Nordhausen, married Marie Genvier (Catholic), from Ranuski/Quebec (possibly Rimouski), on 22 January 1783, at Riviere - Quelle/Quebec.

16. Kiesel, August - Captain-at-arms, Schwarzburg's Company, from Zerbst, married Catherina Peltier (Catholic), from St. Jean/Quebec, on 4 March 1783, at St. Roc/Quebec.

17. Schulze, Christian - Private, Rauschenplat's Company, from Bautzen, married Babosch (?) Vallet (Catholic), from Quebec, on 31 July 1783, at Beaumont/Quebec.

18. Voelker, Conrad - Private, Piquet's Company, married Dorothea Magdalene Bergener, from Hannover, on 30 December 1783, at Jever.

19. Menhold, Christian - Private, Rauschenplat's Company, from Langensalza, married Anna Sophia Jordans, from Varel, on 2 January 1784 at Jever.

20. Lobbes, Johann Gottfried - Lance-corporal, Wietersheim's Company, from Belzig, married Anna Catherina Roewin, from Varel, on 27 January 1784 (at Jever).

21. Hildebrand, Melchior Ulrich - Private, Rauschenplat's Company, from Jever, married Johanna Friederica Anna Baumgarten, from Neustadt-Goedens on 27 January 1784, (at Jever).

22. Schmidt, Wilhelm - Corporal, Piquet's Company, from Halle, married Margaretha Catherina Borgers, from Waddewarden, on 3 February 1784 (at Jever).

23. Moldaner, Johann David - Private, Rauschenplat's Company, from Lehheim in Hesse-Darmstadt, married the widow Bauer, nee Francke, from Berrnburg, in Anhalt, on 3 February 1784 (at Jever).

24. Fischer, David - Sergeant-major, Rauschenplat's Company, from Muehlingen, in Anhalt-Zerbst, married Johanna Margaretha Christiana Danziger, from Jever, on 12 February 1784 (at Jever).

25. Roehrs, Melchior - Private, Piquet's Company, from Backern, in Oldenburg (possibly Backum above Vechta?), married Anna Sophia Elisabeth Wunder, daughter of the deceased regimental drummer, on 12 February 1784 (at Jever).

26. Sattler, Heinrich August - Corporal, Schwarzburg's Company, from Arnstadt, in Schwarzburg, married Catherina Rebecca Oetke, daughter of the deceased baker Remmers Oetke, from Jever, on 24 September 1784 (at Jever).

27. Telz, Johann Friedrich - Lieutenant, (White Regiment), from Roslau, (son of the deceased merchant, August Jacob Telz, from Roslau, married Augusta Carolina von Poellnitz, daughter of the

deceased 1st Lieutenant Friedrich August von Poellnitz, on 30 October 1784, at Jever.

28. Schenk, Gerhard - Corporal, Nuppenau's Company, from Jever, [possibly brother of #8 above], from Jever, married a [Miss] Meyne, daughter of the deceased shoemaker Meyne, from Varel, on 11 November 1784, (at Jever).

29. Goebel, Johann Wilhelm - Battalion Surgeon, (White Infantry Regiment), from Hannover, married Helena Sophia Martens, from Varel, daughter of the master joiner, Heinrich Martens, from Varel, on 18 November 1784, (at Jever).

30. Metzfetzel, Johann Dietrich - Private, Piquet's Company, from Jever, married Boecke (?) Marie Harms, daughter of the castle schoolmaster in Jever, on 20 December 1784, at Jever.

31. Vollhardt, Ludewig - Lieutenant (White Regiment) from Pirmasens (?), son of the deceased Lieutenant Colonel Vollhardt, of the Hesse-Darmstadt service, married Anna Gerdrut Martin, daughter of Captain Johann Martin, of the von Wietersheim Battalion, on 26 December 1784, (at Jever).

Births/Baptisms

1. Matthaes, Johann August* - 23 February 1778, at Brunis, in Saxony, Father: Private Matthaes, (of Schwarzburg's Company.)

2. Packendorf, Johanna Friederica Eleonora - 2/4 April 1778, at Stade, Father: Private Packendorf (of the 1st Grenadier Company).

3. Wenzel, Johann Christian Heinrich - 13 June 1778, on board the transport ship *Present Succession* on the high seas, Father: Private Wenzel (of Schwarz burg's Company).

4. Hensse, Johann Christian Heinrich* - 27 June /27 July 1778, on board the ship *Present Succession*, Father: Private Hensse (of Gogel's Company).

5. Puhlmann, Anna Catharina Friederica* - 18/19 July 1778, on the ship *The Rising Sun,* Father: Private Puhlmann (of Piquet's Company).

6. Andress, Carolina Sophia Margaretha* - 30 August 1778, on board the ship *The Rising Sun*, Father: Private Christian Andress (of Piquet's Company),

7. Family name unknown, Philipp George - 20 September 1778, at Quebec, Father: A butcher's servant for a butcher by the name of Heubsch (who is the sponsor), (The underlining of Georg in the original, in an unknown handwriting, as if it were the

family name, is false. Braunsdorf left an obvious space in the entry.)

8, Wille, Johann Julius George - 21/23 September 1778, at Quebec, Father; Private Wille (of the Brunswick troops).

9. Haberlandt, Carl Ludwig Christian * - 20/22 November 1778, at Quebec, Father: Private Johann Gottfried Haberlandt.

10. Wolf, Susanna Elisabeth - 22/24 July 1779, at Quebec, Father: The butcher Philipp Wolf.

11. Ludewig, Christian Anthon - 3/4 August 1779, at Quebec, Father: Private Anthon Ludewig, a carpenter (in Gogel's Company).

12. Barth(s), Anna Sophia Magdalena* - 20/22 September 1779, at Quebec, Father: Private Johann Friedrich Barth(s) (of Schwarzburg's Company).

13. Krug, Johann Peter*- 26/28 September 1778 [probably should be 1779], at Quebec, Father: Private Krug (of Gogel's Company).

14. Schenk, Johann Christian Carl - 3/5 October 1779, at Quebec, Father: Sergeant-major Schenk (of Piquet's Company).

15. Klinn, Johanna Frederica - baptized 5 November 1779, at St. Francois, by the clergyman Bedard, Father: Private Klinn (of Schwarzburg's Company).

16. Mast, Johann Martin Alexander - 3/7 December 1779, at St. Thomas, by the parish priest, Msr. Mesonbash, Father: Private Mast (of Wietersheim's Company).

17, Matthaes, Friederica Elisabeth - 20/23 December 1779, at St. Pierre/Quebec, Father: Private Mattthaes (of Gogel's Company).

18. Schoell, Carl Friederich von - 12/14 February 1780, at Quebec, (from concubine), Father: Captain von Schoell (of the Hesse-Hanau Regiment), Mother: "a soldier's woman from the Brunswick troops, who lived with him as his mistress."

19. Paul, Christiana Elisabeth* - 16 May 1780, at Quebec, by the English city clergyman, de Montmolin, Father: Private Paul (of Wietersheim's Company).

20. Rogge(ns), Carl Michael Philipp - and

21. Rogge(ns), Johanna Lena (Magdalena) Dorothea (twins) - 17 May 1780, on board ship, on the voyage from New York to Quebec (during the transportation of Brunswick prisoners) - 16 July 1780, in camp at Quebec, Father: Private Carl Rogge(ns), (of the Brunswick troops).

22. Piquet, Maria Elisabeth* - 9/14 June 1780, at Quebec, Father: Brigade-major and Captain (Carl Friedrich) Piquet.

23. Mugge, Johann August Georg Christian -

14/15 June 1780, at Quebec, Father: Private Johann Heinrich Mugge (of Ehrenkrook's Regiment of Brunswick troops).

24. Heydt, Franz - 20/22 June 1780, at St. Thomas, by the clergyman Mesonbash, Father: Private Heydt (of Piquet's Company).

25. Kreyseler, Christiana Catharina* - 2/5 July 1780, at Beauport/Quebec, Father: Private Johann Christian Friedrich Kreyseler, carpenter (of Wietersheim's Company).

26. Ehnen, David Friedrich* - 14/16 September 1780, at Pointe Lewis/Quebec, Father: Private Ehnen (of Gogel's Company).

27. Demmert, Ludwig - 11 October 1780, according to the statement of Valentin Krill, of the 1st [Hesse]-Hanau Jaeger Corps, at the private baptism, on the Isle au Noix/Montreal, on 22/30 January 1780. [This probably should be October, as the German text, by the authors has the date as 22./30.1.1780, and 10/1780 seems more logical.] Father: Private Otto Demmert (of the same unit).

28. Luebben, Johann Friedrich - 2/5 January 1781, at Becancour/Trois Rivieres, Father: Cannoneer Friedrich Luebbens (of the Artilllery Corps).

29. Mauck, Johann Wilhelm - 14/15 October 1780, at Pointe Lewis/Quebec, Father: Jaeger Gottlieb

Mauck (of Count Wittgenstein's Company, of the Hesse-Hanau [Jaeger Corps]).

30. Schroeck, Catharina Eleanora Carolina* - 29 January/1 February 1782, at Becancour/Trois Rivieres, Father: Private Matthaeus Schroeck (of Schwarzburg's Company).

31. Krug, Johanna Magdalena Frederica - 10/12 February 1781, at Nicolet/Trois Rivieres, Father: Private Jacob Krug, (of Gogel's Company).

32. Pressler, Christiana Margaretha - 30 March/1 April 1781, at Becancour/Trois Rivieres, Father: Private Johann Pressler, (of Schwarzburg's Company)

33. Schmidt, Johann Friedrich - 14 April/6 May 1781, at La Bay St. Antoine (by the Catholic priest), Father: Private Schmidt (of Rauschenplat's Company).

34. Puhlmann, Friedrich Carl Bartholomaeus - 23/24 May 1781, at Lac St. Paul/Trois Rivieres, Father: Private Puhlmann (of Piquet's Company).

35. Nuppenau, Friederica Augusta, and

36. Nuppenau, Marie Charles (twins), 28 June/3 July 1781, at Nicolet, Father: Captain-lieutenant (Johann August Zacharias) Nuppenau.

37. Piquet, Philipp Friedrich Carl - 13/17 September 1781, at Becancour/Trois Rivieres, Father: Brigade-major and Captain (Carl Friedrich) Piquet.

38. Packendorf, Catharina Magdalena - 21/23 September 1781, at Becancour/Trois Rivieres, Father: Private Packendorf (of Piquet's Company).

39. Heyderich, Johann Conrad Gottfried - 25/27 September 1781, in La Bay St. Antoine, Father: Private Heyderich (of Rauschenplat's Company).

40. Schenk, Christiana Sophia Elisabeth - 12/16 October 1781, at La Bay St. Antoine/Trois Rivieres, Father: Sergeant-major Schenk (of Schwarzburg's Company).

41. Klinger, Johann August - 3/6 November 1781, at St. Jean/Trois Rivieres, Father: Private Klinger (of Rauschenplat's Company).

42. Ehnen, Jacob Carl Martin Gottfried - 20/25 November 1781, at Lotbiniere/Trois Rivieres, Father: Private Ehnen (of Gogel's Company).

43. Klinge, Johann Friedrich Christoph - 26 November 1781, at St. Jean/Trois Rivieres, by the Catholic Regimental Chaplain Becker, Father: Private Klinge (Catholic) (of Schwarzburg's Company).

44. Ramhorst, Johann Georg Friederich - 15/18 December 1781, at Gentilly, Father: Private Ramhorst, (of Piquet's Company).

45. Kreyseler, Johann Christian Friedrich - 19/21 January 1782, at St. Antoine/Trois Rivieres, Father: Private Kreyseler, carpenter, (of Wietersheim's

Company).

46. Matthaes, Christiana Frederica - 7/8 February 1782, at Lotbiniere/Trois Rivieres, Father: Private Matthaes (of Schwarzburg's Company).

47. Cocks, William - 10 February 1782, at Point aux Trembles/Quebec, Father: Adjutant Cocks (probably Cox) of the English 53rd Regiment.

48. Dogles, Robert - 3 December 1781/25 February 1782, at Point aux Trembles, Father: Private Robert Dogles (probably Douglas) of the English 53rd Regiment.

49. Wolf, Sophia Philippine - 27 June/4 July 1782, at St. Jean/Quebec, Father: Marquetaener [furniture maker?, if the same as the individual in #10 and #60, possibly a butcher], Philip Wolf.

50. Nuppenau, August* - 24/26 October 1782, at Quebec, Father: Captain (Johann August Zacharias) Nuppenau.

51. Hoffmann, Johann Kraft - 25/27 October 1782, at Pointe Lewis/Quebec, Father: Private Gottfried Hoffmann, (of Lentz' Company of the Hesse-Hanau Leib Regiment).

52. Losberger, Dorothea Magdalena - 22 August/28 October 1781, at Long Island/Pointe Lewis, Father: Johannes Losberger, Wagonmaster, in the Hesse-Nassau Artillery Corps.

53. Packendorf, Johanna Sophia - 17/18 November 1782, at St. Anne/Quebec, Father: Private Packendorf, (of Piquet's Company).

54. Heydt, Christian Gottfried Adam - 10/13 February 1783, at Riviere Quellle/Quebec, Father: Private Heydt, hautboist.

55. Schmidt, Anna Catharina Sophia* - 14/16 February 1783, at Riviere Quelle/Quebec, Father: Private Schmidt (of Rauschenplat's Company).

56. Heyderich, Johanna Christiana - 16/21 April 1783, at Riviere Quelle/Quebec, Father: Private Heyderich, (of Rauschenplat's Company).

57. Schroeck, Maria Elisabeth - 20/22 May 1783, at St. Roc/Quebec, Father: Private Schroeck, (of Schwarzburg's Company).

58. Piquet, Catherine Skeene - 12/17 June 1783, at St. Foy/Quebec, by the English clergyman Montmolin, Father: Brigade-major and Captain (Carl Friedrich) Piquet.

59. Ludewig, Maria Catherina - 9/11 July 1783, at Beaumont/Quebec, Father: Private Ludewig, carpenter (of Gogel's Company).

60. Wolff, [sic], Friederich Benjamin Carl Hero - 20/23 August 1783, on board the ship *Hero*, on the return voyage from America to Germany, Father: [see 49 above].

HESSIAN CHAPLAINS

61. Schenk, Friedrich Christian Gerhardt - 3/5 October 1783, at Jever, Father: Sergeant-major Schenk, (of Schwarzburg's Company).

62. Kolbe, Johanna Christina Frederica - 24 November 1783, at Jever, Father: Surgeon's mate Kolbe.

63. Friedrich, Heinrich - 24 November 1783, at Jever, Father: Drummer Martin Friedrich.

64. Nuppenau, Timon Friedrich August - 21/25 February 1784, at Jever, Father: Captain (Johann August Zacharias) Nuppenau.

65. Ehnen, Johanna Sophia Margaretha* - 3/6 April 1784, at Jever, Father: Private Ehnen, (of Nuppenau's Company).

66. Boelken, Christiana Elisabeth - 9/11 September 1784, at Jever, Father: Private Daniel Boelken.

67. Sattler, Catharina Maria - 22/24 September 1784, at Jever, Father: Corporal Sattler, (of Schwarzburg's Company).

68. Family name unknown, Friedrich David - 4 December 1784, at Jever, Mother: the widow of the former Artillery Corporal Ulrich Gerdes; reported Father: Sergeant-major David Braun, (of Nuppenau's Company).

69. Telz, August Friedrich Sigmund - 25/26

December 1784, at Jever, Father: Lieutenant (Johann Friedrich) Telz.

70. Hannemann, Johann Casper - 27/29 December 1784, at Jever, Father: Private Hannemann, (of Wietersheim's Company).

71. Family name unknown, Johann August - 10/11 January 1785, at Jever, Mother: the widow of Cannoneer Wipling, deceased in America, reported Father: Cannoneer Lange.

72, Roehrs, Johann Christian Friedrich* - 18/20 January 1785, at Jever, Father: Private Roehrs, (of Schwarzburg's Company).

73. Hoehne, Friedrich Jacob Franciscus - 28/30 January 1785, at Jever, Father: Private Hoehne, of the 2nd Vacant Company).

74. Hildebrand, Johann Carl - 29/30 January 1785, at Jever, Father: Private Hildebrandt, (of the 2nd Vacant Company).

75. Weber, Maria Sophia - 4/6 March 1785, at Jever, Father: Private David Weber, (of Nuppenau's Company).

76. Schmidt, Catherina Cohra - 30 September/ 2 October 1784, [possibly this should be 1785], at Jever, Father: Corporal Schmidt, (of Wietersheim's Company).

77. Gensch, Friedrich August - 5 April 1785

(private baptism), at Jever, Father: Corporal Gensch, (of Piquet's Company).

78. Giesfeld, Charlotte Dorothea Elisabeth - 6/8 April 1785, at Jever, Father: Lance-corporal Giesfeld, (of the 1st Vacant Company).

79. Goebel, Carl Georg Wilhelm - 14/17 April 1785, at Jever, Father: the appointed Battalion-surgeon Goebel.

80. Peters, Maria Elisabeth - 16/17 April 1785, at Jever, Father: Private Peters, (of Schwarzburg's Company).

81. Hebert [sic], Johann Christian Andres - 20/22 April 1785, at Jever, Father: Private Herbert [sic], (of the 2nd Vacant Company).

82. Schmidt, Johann Heinrich Hermann - 23/24 April 1785, at Jever, Father: Private Schmidt, (of the 2nd Vacant Company).

83. Havenbrack, Johann Wilhelm Anthon - 10/11 May 1785, at Jever, Father: Private Havenbrack, (of Piquet's Company).

84. Heyd(t), Gottlob Bartholomaeus - 14/16 May 1785, at Jever, Father: Heydt, deceased (a quarter of a year previously) (of Piquet's Company). (Hautboist Franz Heyd(t) died on 2 February 1785 at Jever.)

ANSBACH-BAYREUTH
Church Book
Compiled by
Chaplain Stroelein

INTRODUCTION

Ansbach-Bayreuth was one of the six German states which provided England with the so-called "Hessian" auxiliaries during the American Revolutionary War. The chaplains who accompanied the Hessians kept records of religious activities in "Church Books", just as the clerics in Germany kept records of their religious duties.

After the war, an Ansbach chaplain, Pastor Gregorius Michael Stroelein, or possibly, Aroelein, compiled a listing of births in the von Voit, or Ansbach, and the Jaeger Regiments. As the only other Ansbach-Bayreuth unit sent to America, was the Bayreuth Regiment, and as it was stationed in Bayreuth after the war, Chaplain Stroelein possibly did not have access to that unit's church book. Therefore, the following translation does not list births in the Bayreuth Regiment, nor are deaths nor weddings, which are usually included in the church books, listed in Chaplain Stroelein's church book.

The manuscript copy of the book from which I worked is maintained in the Landeskirchliches Archiv, Zentrale Kirchenbuchstelle, Am Oelberg 2, 84oo Regensburg, Germany. Some of the writing is extremely difficult to decipher, and as a result, there may be errors in my translation.

However, my translation is easier to read than the Old German script. In making my translation, I have used an e after the vowels a, o, and u to indicate when the vowels were umlauted. I have also used a question mark, in brackets, at times, when I was unsure of the preceding word. In a few cases, I have supplied additional interpreting information, usually from Erhard Staedtler's Die Ansbach-Bayreuther Truppen in Amerikanisches Unabhaengigkeitskrieg, 1777-1783, (Nuernberg, 1956), However, I have not always agreed with Staedtler's spelling of all proper names, based on how I deciphered the writing in the manuscript, and his obvious reference to the same persons.

In making the English translation, I have taken certain liberties in changing the format, phrasing, and sentence structures. I have tried not to alter the meaning of any portion of the script.

I noted only two of the mothers as being American women, but there was also one American woman, the wife of Captain Moritz Wilhelm von der Heyde, who was a sponsor, and David Grimm, father of one of the mothers, was a New York innkeeper, whose establishment is mentioned in many "Hessian" diaries of the period.

I hope my efforts will provide some additional

knowledge, not only about the founding of our nation, but also about the people who participated in the event. As always, I suggest that serious students return to the original document to verify my work.

Bruce E. Burgoyne
Dover, DE
December 1991

Ansbach-Bayreuth Church Book
Pastor Georgius Michael Stroelein, Year 1783

A listing of the children of the Voit Infantry Regiment, some of whom were baptized in North America, some on the journey, on water and on land, prepared by me, the Lutheran Chaplain Stroelein, based on certificates, and where these are missing, by word of mouth of the parents, and recorded as a pastor's duty.

Note: As is known, two regiments (of the so-called battalions), those of the Jaeger and the Voit Infantry Regiments, returned home from America, and were joined together. Chaplain G[eorg] Christ[oph] Fr. Erb, returned with the Jaeger Regiment. He gave me a written true copy extract of all the baptisms he had performed, most of which I have included here, as confirmed.

[Johann Christoph] Wagner, chaplain of the Ansbach Infantry Regiment, remained behind in North America, because he was promised great benefits. Therefore, I have had to collect all the proper baptisms, with some effort, and obtain information from the sergeants of all the companies, concerning the individuals under their supervision, so that the barracks baptismal register, under my official direction should have no errors, and my successor would not have the responsibility.

1778 - On 4 July, at nine o'clock at night, there was born on Long Island, in America, and thereafter baptized:

1. Hunigunda Barbara - the father is Balthasar Scheerer, grenadier of Captain [Christian Philipp] von Ellrodt's Company. The mother's name is Mar. Apolloma, nee Hesslein. Sponsor: Hunigunda Barbara Pehl, wife of Musketeer Pehl, of Colonel von Voit's Company.

1778 - At twelve o'clock at night, on 18 August there was born at New York, in North America, and on 23 August, baptized:

2. Georg Ernst - the small, legitimate son of Quartermaster Sergeant Johann Georg Friederich Schnalz, of the von Voit Ansbach Infantry Regiment, and his wife, Maria Elisabeth Catharina. Sponsors: Sergeant Jacob Ernst Kling, and Quartermaster Sergeant Johann Georg Beck, both of the Ansbach Field Jaeger Corps.

Note: In the absence of Chaplain Wagner, this child was verified by me, as having been baptized by F. [Karl] Becker, the Reformed Staff Chaplain, of the Hessian Relief Corps.

1779. On 8 March, at Newport, Rhode Island, there was legitimately born, and thereafter baptized, by Chaplain Wagner:

1. Johann Friederich - the father is Georg Sirtus Gebauer, private in Major von Ellrodt's Company. The mother's name is Anna Sibylla, nee Pulzor. Sponsor: Johann Friederich Hauf, former sergeant of that company.

1782 - At eight o'clock at night, on 24 February, at New York, there was born and baptized:

2. Johann Mathias Wolfgang - the small, legitimate son of Mathias Ruethner, carpenter of Colonel von Voit's Company, and his wife, Eva, nee Poeberl. Sponsor was Johann Georg Wolfgang Stachsoefen [?], servant of Colonel von Voit, at that time.

1782 - On 20 September, between midnight and one o'clock in the morning, there was born and baptized:

3. Margaretha Barbara - in the camp at King's Bush, five English miles from New York. The father is Johann Neff, field jaeger of Captain von [Friedrich Wilhelm] Roeder's Company, of the Evangelical faith. The mother is Wilhelmina, nee Sittmann, of the Catholic faith. Regimental witness of the baptism was Margaretha Barbara Rummel, wife of Field Jaeger

Christian Conrad Rummel.

1782 - At two in the afternoon of 3 October, there was legitimately born, and therefore baptized:

1. Ernst Friedrich - the father is Georg Chateau, of Meissenheim, in Saarbruecken, a corporal in the Jaeger Regiment. The mother is Anna Maria, nee Buettner, of Ansbach. Sponsor: Captain Ernst Friederich Wilhelm von Wurmb, of that regiment, who died of a wound received during action at Penobscot.

1782 - At three o'clock in the afternoon of 17 December, there was legitimately born, at Penobscot, and thereafter baptized:

2. Michael Peter - the father is Georg Arnold, a field jaeger from Ansbach: the mother, Margaretha, nee Wunderlich, of Bayreuth. Sponsors: Vice-corporal Michael Peter Krieger and his wife Elisabeth.

1782 - at Penobscot, at five o'clock in the morning of 30 December, there was legitimately born, and thereafter baptized:

3. Anna Regina Elisabeth - the father is Field Jaeger Georg Rosenhauer, from Culmbach; the mother is Elisabeth, nee Schweigen, of M. Erlbach. Sponsors: Field Jaeger Georg Jakob Schurpf, and his wife, Anna Regina Elisabeth.

1783 - on 29 January, at Norwich, on Long Island, there was legitimately born, and due to an absence of clergy, only on 12 May 1783 , baptized:

4. Miss Esther Harriette Catharina - the father is Captain [Christoph Friedrich Joseph] von Waldenfels, of this regiment; mother, Mistress Sarah von Waldenfels, nee Forgon. Sponsors: 1) Mistress Hedwig von der Heyde, wife of Captain [Moritz Wilhelm] von der Heyde, nee Hopson, and 2) Frau Anna Catharina Bach, wife of Lieutenant [Joseph] Bach, nee Stiegler.

1783 - on 24 July, at Harlem, on York [Manhattan] Island, there was legitimately born, and thereafter baptized:

9) Johann Martin - the father is Tobias Wolff, field jaerger; the mother, Anna Regina, nee Weyh. Sponsors: Corporal Nikolaus Stoehr, and Corporal Johann Martin.

On the Return Voyage from America
On Board the Ship *South Carolina*

1783 - On 9 August, there was legitimately born, and on 11 August, baptized:

10. Carl Lorenz - the father is Conrad Hager, field jaeger; the mother, Nancy, nee MacDonald, of County Edinburg, in Scotland. Sponsor: Corporal Carl Lorenz Hering. The child was named Carl as a

reminder of the ship's name.

1783 - at ten o'clock in the morning, on 2 September, aboard the same ship, there was legitimately born, and thereafter baptized:

11. Johanna Maria Carolina and Johann Carl Friederich - the father is Johann Thomas Lindner, field jaeger sergeant; the mother Johanna Catharina, nee Seiss, of Dorflas. Sponsors: 1) Carl Friederich Neuss [?], surgeon of the same regiment, and 2) Johanna Maria Sabina Pausch, nee Engelhardt, of Ansbach, wife of Jaeger Sergeant [Johann Michael] Pausch.

Note: The boy was named after the ship's captain, John Brown; the girl after the frigate *[South] Carolina.*

1783 - at three o'clock, in the afternoon, of 15 July, at Penobscot, during the absence of the chaplain, there was born, after the Ansbach troops were reunited at The Downs (England), baptized aboard the ship, *The Brothers,* on 8 September:

5. Anna Susanna - the legitimate daughter of Field Jaeger Johann Conrad Hasster, and his wife, Catharina Margaretha, nee Trips. Sponsor: Anna Susanna, from Rastal [?], wife of the Hunting Horn-player Schramm.

1783 - on 15 May, in the absence of Chaplain Erb, there was born at Penobscot, and on 8 September, baptized:

6. Johann Friederich - the legitimate son of Field Jaeger Georg Adam Benz, and his wife, Marion, nee Winter, of Fuerth. Sponsor: Field Jaeger Friederich Neues [?], from Schwabach,

1783 - on 27 September, on the return march, at Bremen, there was born, and on 2 October, baptized:

7. Johann Friederich - the legitimate son of Joseph Carl Wildscheck, hunting horn-player, from Jucay, in Hungary, and his wife, Helena Henrika, nee Koenig. Sponsor: Johann Heinrich Lachs, hunting horn-player.

1783 - at eleven o'clock at night, on 23 September, there was born at Bremen, in the absence of a military chaplain, and on 29 October at Hannover Muenden, baptized:

8. Johann Ludwig - the legitimate son of Artillerist Johann Georg Weber, of the von Voit Infantry Regiment, and his wife, Regina, nee Ahold, from Frederick, [Maryland], in North America. Sponsor: Private Johann Ludwig Heckert, of that regiment.

1783 - on 19 October, on board the frigate *Auerbach* [?], on the North Sea, there was born, and on 29 October, baptized, by Superintendent Stockenesel, at Hannover Muenden:

1. Maria Margaretha - the legitimate daughter of Musketeer Mathias Walther, of the von Voit Infantry Regiment, and his wife, Regina Barbara, nee Schwenohl. Sponsor: Corporal Weinberger's wife, Maria Margaretha.

6 November 1783 - at Michels Kumbach, in the Bishopric of Fulda, there was legitimately born, and thereafter baptized:

2. Johanna Catharina Friederika - the father is Field Jaeger Dominicus Valentin; the mother is Elisabeth, nee Reiss. Sponsor: Johanna Catharina Frederika, wife of Sergeant [Johann Thomas] Lindner, also of that regiment.

On 9 November 1783 - at three o'clock in the morning, at Mitgefeld, in Fulda, there was legitimately born, and thereafter at Pfastenhausen, in Fulda, baptized:

3. Johann Georg - the son of Field Jaeger Nikolaus Popp, and his wife, Anna Margaretha, nee Gerst. This was confirmed by Sergeant Johann Georg Hannecker, of the Jaeger Regiment.

According to the enclosed statement from the father in New York, in America, there was born on 21 August 1782:

HESSIAN CHAPLAINS

4. Maria Carolina - the father is Johann Andreas Carl von Stein zu Altenstein; the mother is Maria Elisabeth, nee Grimm, both Evangelical. On 4 September, this child was baptized at New York, with David Grimm, merchant in New York, the father of the dear mother, in attendance. Sponsors: Carl Heinrich von Stein zu Altenstein, grandfather on the paternal side, Ansbach colonel and commandant at Erlangen, and his wife, Sophia Charlotta von Altenstein, nee von Roth.

Enclosure

My daughter, Maria Carolina, was born on 21 August 1782, and baptized fourteen days later. Sponsors: My father, Colonel von Stein zu Altenstein; my mother, Sophia Carolina Charlotta von Stein zu Altenstein, nee von Roth; and my father-in-law, David Grimm, merchant in New York, in America.

/S/ v. Altenstein

INDEX

----, Friedrich David 129 Georg 121
  Jacob 16 Johann August 130
  Philipp George 121
ABEL, Arietha Martha Elisabeth 4
  Catharina 4 Christoph 4
ACHMEYER, Friedrich Conrad 43
  Wilhelmina Leonora 43
ACKERMANN, Karen 13
ADAMS, Johann 80
AHOLD, Regina 142
ALBERS, Heinrich 91
ALHAUS, Anna Rebecka 37 Johann
  Ernst 37 Wilhelm Justus 36
ALMEROTH, Egidia 58 Friedrich 58
  Georg 58
ALTENSTEIN, Carl Heinrich Von
  Stein Zu 144 Col Von Stein Zu
  144 Johann Andreas Carl Von
  Stein Zu 144 Maria Carolina 144
  Maria Elisabeth 144 Sophia
  Carolina Charlotta Von Stein Zu
  144
AMBROSIUS, Anna Dorothea 38
  Elisabeth 39 Johann Daniel 39
AMELUNG, Senior Surgeon 41
AMTHAUER, Anna Catharina 32
  Reitze 32
ANDRESS, Carolina Sophia
  Margaretha 70 121 Christian 70
  121
APFEL, Adam 101
APT, Anna Dorothea 49 Friedrich 49
ARNOLD, Georg 139 Margaretha 139
  Michael Peter 139
AROELEIN, Gregorius Michael 133
ASSEMANN, Elisabeth 23
AUERBACH, Christoph 87
AUG, Susanna 11
AULBEL, Catherina Elisabeth 24
BACH, Anna Catharina 140 Joseph
  140
BAER, Christian 79
BAETGE, Friederich 77

BALLE, August 68
BARTH, Anna Sophia Magdalena 122
  Johann Friedrich 122
BARTHEL, Anna Catherina 11
  Martha Elisabeth 11 Nicolaus 11
BARTHS, Anna Sophia Magdalena
  122 Johann Friedrich 115 122
  Maria Dorothea 115
BARTHSEN, Anna Sophia
  Magdalena 98
BAUER, Andrea 88 Johann Georg 9
  Widow 119
BAUMGARTEN, Adam 77 Johanna
  Friederica Anna 118
BAURMEISTER, Maj 31 33
BAYEUX, Catharina Charlotta 42
  Cornelia 43 Mr 43
BECK, Johann Georg 137
BECKER, Anna Christina 8 37
  Chaplain 126 F Karl 137
BEDARD, 122
BENCKE, Friederich 78
BENZ, Georg Adam 142 Johann
  Friederich 142 Marion 142
BERGENER, Dorothea Magdalene
  118
BERGER, Jacob 97
BERGES, Johann 66
BERGHOLZ, Christian 76
BERNHARD, Charlotte 19 Michael
  19
BIERHENNE, Anna Martha 41
  Conrad 41 Henrich 41
BILANGER, Marie Therese 117
BLEICH, Gottfried 79
BLESEN, Capt 16
BLUM, Christoph 23 Elisabeth 10
  Maria Catherina 12 Samuel 12
BODE, Capt 21
BOELKEN, Christiana Elisabeth 129
  Daniel 129
BOLT, Elisabeth 12
BOMBERG, Christoph 80

BONNIUS, Friederich 85
BORCK, Georg 22
BORGERS, Margaretha Catherina 118
BOULANGER, Anna Catharina 50 Christina 50 Nicolaus 50
BRAND, Elizabeth Christina 45 Regina 50
BRANDENBURG, Maria Catharina 48
BRANDT, And 74 Andreas 71 Corp 78 Johann Gottlieb 74 Mrs 71
BRANDTIN, Maria Catharina 78
BRAUN, Anna Catherina 14 21 David 129
BRAUNSDORF, 111 113 122 Chaplain 65 97 110 Christina W 114 Christina Wilhelmina 113 Franz Siegismund Wilhelm 113-114 Johann Gottlieb Siegismund 62-63 110 112 Johann Gottlieb Siergismund 113 Johanna 114
BRETHAUER, Johann Henrich 23
BRETKER, Johann Christian 117 Marie Magdalene 117
BRIENING, Johanna Elizabeth 115
BROWN, John 141
BUETTNER, Anna Maria 139
BUHLMANN, Sophia 117
BURSCHEL, Johann 16 Sophia 16
BUSCH, Friedrich 17 Wilhelmina Catherina 17
CARTEUSER, Andreas 34
CASPAR, Ehrhardt 67
CHATEAU, Anna Maria 139 Ernst Friedrich 139 Georg 139
CHEMNITZ, Christian Gottfried 113 Christina W 114 Christina Wilhelmina 113 Johann Ludwig 113 Miss 113 Sophie Wilhelmina 113
CHRISTIAN, Berthold 12
CLAUS, Dorothea 46
CLAUSING, Ludwig 17 Wilhelmina Catherina 17
COCKS, Adj 127 William 127
COESTER, Chaplain 58 G C 2 Georg C 3

COJE, Adam 70 Anna Catharina 69 Maria Christiana 79 Pvt 79
COMPHIEL, Samuel 46
COX, Adj 127
COZINE, Margaretha 32 Mr 32
CRASS, Anna Catherina 116 Johann 66
CROSS, Anna Catherina 116
DANIEL, Carl 73
DANZIGER, Johanna Margaretha Christina 119
DECKER, Justus 22
DELALIME, Charlotte 19
DEMMERT, Ludwig 124 Otto 124
DEMONTMOLIN, 123
DESCOURDES, Louis 43
DICKHAUT, Anna Gerdruth 54 Henrich Reinhard 54 Johannes 49 Leonora Luisa 15 Werner 15 54
DIETERICH, 73
DIETRICH, Elisabeth 39 Jacob 32 Maria Margaretha 32 Martha Catharina 32
DIETZEL, Lt 44 Mrs 44
DITMAR, Anna Elisabeth 57 Catharina Elisabeth 28 Johann Wilhelm 28
DOENSTAEDT, Anna Martha 41
DOGLES, Robert 127
DOUGLAS, Robert 127
DRONT, Christian 95
DUITTGEN, Bernhard 70
DUPUY, Maj 40-41
EBERHARD, David 45 Dorothea Elisabeth 29 45 Johann Valentin 45
EBERT, Johannes 46 Maria Elisabeth 46
EHNEN, David Friederich 109 David Friedrich 124 Jacob Carl Martin Gottfried 126 Johanna Sophia Margaretha 108 129 Pvt 108-109 124 126 129
EHRENKROOK, 124
EICHENAUER, Anton 38
EICHLER, Elizabeth 55
EICHLERS, Elisabeth 29 Jost 29
EISMANN, Margaretha 8

EITEL, Hans Heinrich 32 Lt Col 51
EMLOTH, Anna Elisabeth 53
    Johannes 53
ENGELHARD, Christian 26 Eva
    Barbara 26 Johann Valentin 26
ENGELHARDT, Johanna Maria
    Sabina 141
ERB, Chaplain 142 Dorothea
    Elisabeth 7 Georg Christoph Fr
    136
EWALD, Capt 49-50 Johann 10
FALKENER, Mrs 27
FEHR, Johann Georg 22
FERBER, Jacob 75
FISCHER, Christoph 83 David 119
    Gottlob 85 Heinrich 73 Johanna
    Margaretha Christina 119 Peter 84
FISTER, Heinrich 85
FLACHSHAAR, Anna Gertruth 40
    Wilhelm 40
FLAMMER, Jacob 71
FOCK, Annette Luzie Margaretha 43
    Georg Henrich 43 Maria Catharina
    43
FORGON, Sarah 140
FRANCKE, 119
FRERICHS, Johann 85
FRERICS, Oldmann 89
FRESDORFF, Peter 83
FREY, Anna Margaretha 25 45
    Conrad 25 Elisabeth Christina 45
    Georg Adolf 25 Georg Adolph 45
    53 Johann Georg 53 Margaretha
    53
FREYTAG, Georg 34 Gerdruth 34
    Johann Caspar 34
FRIEDERICK, Maria Catherina 25
FRIEDMANN, Joseph 86
FRIEDRICH, Heinrich 129 Martin
    129
FRISE, David 8
FRITZ, Ferdinand 94
FUCHS, Maria Sabina 14 Pastor 14
    Wilhelm Dietrich 66
FUEHRER, Carl Friedrich 43
FUELLGRAFF, Anna Gerdruth 47
    Gerhard 47 Johannes 47

GASSERT, Eva Catharina 28 Joseph
    28 Kilian 28
GEBAUER, Anna Sibylla 138 Georg
    Sirtus 138 Johann Friederich 138
GEBHARD, Anna Catharina 45
GEMELING, 20
GENSCH, Corp 131 Friedrich August
    130
GENVIER, Marie 117
GEORGE III, King of England 112
GERDES, Ulrich 72 129
GERST, Anna Margaretha 143
GIESE, Conrad 20
GIESFELD, Charlotte Dorothea
    Elisabeth 131 Lance-corp 131
GLEIM, Anna Elisabeth 57 Elisabeth
    57 Johannes 57
GOEBEL, Capt 30 Carl Georg
    Wilhelm 131 Helena Sophia 120
    Johann Wilhelm 120 Surgeon 131
GOERICKE, Christian 88
GOERKE, Casimir Theodor 19 31
    Elisabeth 20 31 Henrietta 31
GOGEL, 121-126 128 Capt 66-67 69
    71 74 77-78 80 83 83 87-89 92 94
    98 102-104
GOTTLOB, Johannes Franziscus 46-
    47
GRACHELITZ, Gottfried 73
GRAGES, Dorothea Elisabeth 36
    Johann Henrich 36 Sophia
    Wilhelmina 36
GRAMMOND, Marie Magdalene 117
GRASHOFF, Christian 89
GRIMM, David 134 144 Maria
    Elisabeth 144
GROMANN, Dorothea Elisabeth 9
    Johannes 9
GRONEBERG, Georg 79
GROSZ, Conrad 45 Johanna
    Margaretha 45
GRUBER, Jacob 83
GUEMBELL, Anna Elisabeth 10 13
    53-54 54 Philipp 10 13 53
GUISE, Anton 31
HAAK, Corp 36 Sophia Wilhelmina
    36

HABBER, Johann Jost 22
HABERLAND, Gottfried 115
   Johanna Elizabeth 115
HABERLANDT, Carl Ludewich
   Christian 82 Carl Ludwig
   Christian 122 Gottfried 82 Johann
   Gottfried 122
HAEMER, Hamilton Carl Henrich 3
   Johannes 3 15 Maria Elisabeth 15
   Martha Elisabeth 3
HAGER, Carl Lorenz 140 Conrad 140
   Nancy 140
HAMILTON, William 3
HANCK, Maria Wilhelmina 55
   Wilhelmina 29
HANCKEN, Maria Wilhelmina 42
HANNCHEN, Johanna 114
HANNECKER, Johann Georg 143
HANNEMANN, Johann Casper 130
   Pvt 130
HANSTEIN, Capt 17
HARMS, Boecke Marie 120
   Friederich 80 Georg Christian 101
   Heinrich 105 Henrich 66
HARS, Anna Elisabeth 14 53
HARTMANN, Anna Elisabeth 9
   Christina 9 Christoph 103 Jacob 9
HARTUNG, Caspar 86
HARTWIG, Anna Catharina 31 Eva
   Catharina Sophia 31 Johann
   Friedrich 31
HASE, Anna Elisabeth 9 Conrad 9
   Johann Georg 9 Johann George 9
HASELBACH, Elisabeth 26
HASS, Johann Heinrich 99
HASSANPFLUG, Catherina
   Elisabbeth 5 Johann 5
HASSENPFLUG, Anna Catharina 36
   Conrad 36
HASSTER, Anna Susanna 141
   Catharina Margaretha 141 Johann
   Conrad 141
HAUCKE, Gottfried 74
HAUF, Johann Friederich 138
HAUSKNECHT, Chaplain 4
HAVENBRACK, Johann Wilhelm
   Anthon 131 Pvt 131
HAYNLAIN, Anna Catharina 25

HAYNLAIN (continued)
   Georg 25 Maria Catherina 25
HEBERT, Johann Christian Andres
   131 Pvt 131
HECKERT, Johann Ludwig 142
HEIDENRICH, Friedrich 57
HEIDMUELLER, Johann Justus 37
HEINBECK, Anna Catharina 51
   Daniel 51 Johannes Stephan 51
HELLER, Chaplain 11
HELMERICH, Georg Wilhelm 37
HELMICH, Gertrud 12
HEMCE, David 8 Johann Reinhard 8
   Margaretha 8
HENCKELMANN, Barbara 71 Veit
   71
HENCKLEIN, Maria Catharina 37
HENKELMANN, Veit 78-79 Viet 82
HENKELMANNIN, Barbara 78
HENNIG, Ludewich 67
HENSCHEL, Anna Barbara 52
   Eusebrius Eremeteich 52 Johanna
   Rosina Justina 52
HENSSE, Johann Christian Heinrich
   121 Pvt 121
HENTZE, Johann Heinrich 79 Pvt 79-
   80
HENTZIN, Maria Elisabeth 80
HERBERT, Johann Christian Andres
   131 Pvt 131
HERD, Anna Elisabeth 5
HERDMANN, Johann Valentin 26
HERING, Carl Lorenz 140
HERMANN, Anna Catharina 33 Corp
   33
HERRMANN, Andreas 103
HESSE, Wilhelm 81
HESSEMUELLER, Capt 37
HESSLEIN, Mar Apolloma 137
HESSLER, Anna Catharina 14
   Johannes 14 21 Marie Catherina
   21
HEUBSCH, 121
HEYD, Abel 77 Franz 109
HEYD(T), Gottlob Bartholomaeus
   131 Hautboist Franz 131
HEYDERICH, Christopher 115
   Dorothea Maria 115

HEYDERICH (continued)
  Johann Conrad Gottfried 126
  Johanna Christiana 128 Pvt 126 128
HEYDERICHS, Christoph 92
HEYDT, Christian Gottfried Adam 128 Franz 124 Pvt 124 128
HEYMEL, Auditor 17 Col 14 14 28 32 53-54 Karl Philipp 3 Lt Col 3 14
HEYNE, Johann August 97
HILDEBRAND, Johanna Friederica Anna 118 Melchior Ulrich 118
HILDEBRANDT, Johann Carl 130 Pvt 130
HILLBERGT, Andreas 87
HINDERICHS, Christoph 96 Wilhelm 69
HINTE, Col 23 41 Maj 4 13-14
HIRSCH, Anna Margaretha 28 Catharina Elisabeth 28 Conrad 28
HOEHNE, Friedrich Jacob Franciscus 130 Pvt 130
HOFFER, Anton 38 Catharina Elisabeth 38 Johann Henrich 38
HOFFMAN, Johann 107
HOFFMANN, Christian 97 Gottfried 127 Johann Albrecht 117 Johann Kraft 127 Marie Therese 117
HOHENSTEIN, Capt 22 38
HOLZAPFEL, Johann 21
HOLZMUELLER, Christoph 46 Dorothea 46 Johannes Franziscus 46
HOPSON, Hedwig 140
HOYER, Christopher 74
HUENE, Henrich Gottfried 10
HUETHER, Elizabeth Christina 45 Friedrich 45
HUMBURG, Anna Maria 48 Christoph 10 Elisabeth 10 Henrich Wilhelm 10 Valentin 45
HUND, Anna Gerdruth 40 Conrad 40 Martha Catharina 40
HUNDSTOCK, Heinrich 81
HUNOLD, Philipp 41
IDE, Anna Elisabeth 14 Johannes 14
IFFER, Jost Henrich 37

IFFERT, Catherina Elisabeth 8 Johann 8 Johann Henrich 37 Maria Catharina 37 Valentin 37
IHNEN, Heinrich 68
JACOB, Anna Martha 13 Anna Rosina 40 Dillmann 39 Wilhelm Philipp 39
JACOBI, Capt-at-arms 103 Catharina Friderica 35 Friderica Rosina 35 Friedrich Ludwig 35
JACOBIN, Christiana Margaretha 103
JAHN, Christoph 76
JANSSEN, Johann 98
JANTZEN, Wilhellm 87
JNAUST, Gottfried 67
JOHANN, Christoph 95
JORDANS, Anna Sophia 118
KAHLSTUETZER, Eva Barbara 26
KALB, Philipp 99
KATZ, Johannes 30
KATZMANN, Eva 30 51 Johann Caspar 34 Johannes Caspar 30
KAUFHOLD, Anna Catharina 51
KAYSER, Joseph 81
KEHL, Henrich 14 Maria Sabina 14
KELLAIN, Maria Dorothea 115
KERSTING, Johann Christian 39
KIESEL, August 117 Catherina 117 Christian 87
KILLEN, Conrad 21
KIP, Eva 51 Gottfried 51 Martha Catharina 51
KLEE, Kilian 28
KLEINSCHMIDT, Gerdruth 34
KLING, Jacob Ernst 137
KLINGE, Johann Friedrich Christoph 126 Pvt 126
KLINGENDER, Friedrich 50
KLINGER, Johann August 126 Pvt 126
KLINN, Johanna Frederica 122 Pvt 122
KLOESNECK, Heinrich 96
KOCH, Adam Sr 8 Andreas 115 Berthold 12 Grenadier 21 Maria Dorothea 8 Sophia 115 Wilhelm Philipp 8
KOEHLER, Ludewich 77 Martin 72

KOENIG, Christian 68 Helena
 Henrika 142 Johann Heinrich 117
 Marie 117
KOERBEL, Eva Elisabeth 48
KOLBE, Johanna Christina Frederica
 129 Surgeon's Mate 129
KOTENKAMPF, Heinrich 78
KRAMER, Johann Henrich 21
KRAUSE, Christian 11 Friederich 95
KREYSELER, Christiana Catharina
 124 Johann Christian Friedrich
 124 126 Pvt 126
KREYSELERIN, Christiana Catharina
 95 Pvt 95
KRIEGER, Elisabeth 139 Michael
 Peter 139
KRILL, Valentin 124
KRUECK, Anna Catharina 7 Henrich
 56 Johann 7 Johannes 56
KRUESCHEL, Maria Amalia 48 Otto
 Friedrich 48
KRUG, Jacob 125 Johann Peter 89
 122 Johanna Magdalena Frederica
 125 Pvt 89 122
KUEMMELL, Chaplain 57
KUNIGUNDE, Anna 31
KURZ, Anna Catharina 29 49 Anna
 Catherina 6 12 15 25 Joachim 5 15
 25 29 49 Johann 12 Johann Adam
 5 11 Johann Henrich 49
KUTZLEBEN, 21
LACJS, Johann Heinrich 142
LALIME, Jean Baptiste 19
LANDAU, Christina 9
LANGE, Cannoneer 130
LAROSCH, Gottfried 86
LEIN, Johann 91
LEISNER, Maria Catharina 43
LEITHEISER, Friederich 86
LENTZ, 127 Elisabeth 35 Johannes 35
LETZERICH, Johann 16 Martha 16
LEYTMEIER, Rosina Charlotta 18
LINDAUER, 93 Christoph 92
LINDNER, Johann Carl Friederich
 141 Johann Thomas 141 143
 Johanna Catharina 141 Johanna
 Catharina Friederika 143 Johanna
 Maria Carolina 141

LINNINGER, Eva Catharina 28
LIST, Anna Catharina 69 Christopher
 70
LOBBES, Anna Catharina 118 Johann
 Gottfried 118
LOCKBERGER, Anna Christina 50
 Christian 50 Johannes 50
LOEHLER, Abraham 17 Elisabeth 17
LOHR, Maria Elisabeth 15 Martha
 Elisabeth 3
LOREY, Johann Friedrich Henrich 38
LOSBERGER, Dorothea Magdalena
 127 Johannes 127
LOSCH, Anna Maria 49
LUDEWIG, Anna Magdalena 115
 Anthon 98 115 122 Christian
 Anthon 122 Maria Catherina 128
 Pvt 128
LUDING, Johann 107
LUDOLPH, Carl 18 Rosina Charlotta
 18
LUDWIG, Gertruth Sophie 13
 Reinhart 13
LUEBBEN, Friedrich 124 Johann
 Friedrich 124
LUMPE, Johannes 6
MACDONALD, Nancy 140
MAERTHEN, Andreas 33 Anna
 Gerdruth 33 Henrich 33
MANGOLD, Anna Catharina 45
 Franz Christoph 45 Johanna
 Margaretha 44
MARTENS, Heinrich 120 Helena
 Sophia 120
MARTIN, Anna Gerdrut 120
 Catharina 4 Johann 120 140
MAST, Johann Martin Alexander 123
 Paul 99 Pvt 123
MASTIN, Dorothea Sophia 99
MATERN, Heinrich 100
MATTHAES, Christiana Frederica
 127 Friederica Elisabeth 123
 Jacob 104 Johann Andreas 82
 Johann August 121 Pvt 121 123
 127
MAUCK, Gottlieb 124-125 Johann
 Wilhelm 124
MAY, Anna Catharina 36 Christina 50

MAY (continued)
　Galenus 43 Johann Galenus 36
　Wilhelmina Leonora 36 43
MAYER, Eva 30
MEIEN, 17 Sophia 16
MENHOLD, Anna Sophia 118
　Christian 118
MENTZLER, Anna Catharina 51
　Jacob 51
MERTEN, Anna Gertruth 19 Henrich 18
MESONBASH, Msr 123
METZFETZEL, Boecke Marie 120
　Johann Dietrich 120
MEYNE, Carl Friederich 100 Miss 120
MICHALECK, Matthias 106
MICHOLAU, Anthon 87
MINNIGERODE, 22
MOHR, Barbara Elisabeth 41 Conrad 41 Philippus 41
MOLDANER, Johann David 119
MONTMOLIN, 128 Chaplain 116
MOOS, Reinhardt 71
MORITZ, Dorothea Elisabeth 36
MUELLER, Erdmann 68 Wilhelm 107
MUENSTER, Anna Maria 40
MUGGE, Johann August Georg
　Christian 123 Johann Heinrich 124
MURRAY, 25
NAUMANN, Bernhard 27
NEFF, Johann 138 Margaretha
　Barbara 138 Wilhelmina 138
NETZ, Maria Magdalena 8
NETZE, Sgt 8
NEUES, Friederich 142
NEUHAUS, Johann 74
NEUMANN, Capt 38
NEUSS, Carl Friederich 141
NOHR, Anna Magdalena 115
　Dorothea Maria 115
NOHRE, Georg 99
NUMME, Conrad 25
NUPPENAU, 120 130 August 106
　127 Capt 105-106 108-109
　Friederica Augusta 125 Johann
　August Zacharias 116 125 127

NUPPENAU (continued)
　129 Marie 116 Marie Charles 125
　Timon Friedrich 129
OBERSTEIG, Maria Magdalena 11
OELRICHS, Johann 72
OETKE, Catherina Rebecca 119
　Remmers 119
OHM, Wilhelmina Catherina 17
OHNEN, Reinhardt 83
ONCKEN, Heer 103 106
ONKEN, Hajo Eden 82
OPFER, Conrad 54
ORTHWEIN, Anna Barbara 52
OSTERMANN, Christoph 84
OSTHEIM, Johannes 42
OSTWALD, 57
OTTO, Angelica Dorothea 7 Anna
　Catherina 7 Johann Henrich 7
PACKENDORF, Catharina
　Magdalena 126 Johanna
　Friederica Eleonora 121 Johanna
　Sophia 128 Pvt 121 126 128
PATTERSON, Sarah 27 Stephan 27
PAUER, Isabella 58 Mary 58 Merry 58 Thomas 58
PAUL, Abraham 108 Christiana
　Elisabeth 123 Pvt 94 123
PAULIN, Christiana Elisabeth 94
PAULY, Catharina Elisabeth 26
　Elisabeth 26 Johann Dietrich 26
PAUSCH, Johann Michael 141
　Johanna Maria Sabina 141
PAUUER, Isabella 58
PEACOCK, Robert 4
PEHL, Hunigunda Barbara 137
　Musketeer 137
PELOTROW, Maria Elisabeth 46
PELTIER, Catherina 117
PETERS, Maria Elisabeth 131 Pvt 131
PFAFF, Johann Adam 50 52
PFLUEGER, 29 Anna Elisabeth 13 54
　Elisabeth 57 Johann 24
PHEIL, Conrad 33 Martha Catharina 32-33
PICKHARD, Anna Catharina 15 Anna
　Gerdruth 54
PICQUET, Capt 108
PILTZ, Gottfried 69

PIQUET, 115-116 118-119 121-122 124 126 128 131 Capt 66 68 70 72-74 76 79 81-82 84-86 86 93-97 99 99-100 103 106 106 109 Carl Friedrich 116 123 125 128 Catherine Skeene 128 Maria Elisabeth 94 123 Philipp Friedrich Carl 125
PLAUMENS, Elisabeth 58
POEBERL, Eva 138
POPP, Anna Margaretha 143 Johann Georg 143 Nikolaus 143
POST, Anna 31 Anton 30 Georg 30
PREISS, Johann 72 Juliana Dorothea 116
PRESSLER, Christiana Margaretha 125 Johann 125
PRUESCHENCK, Maj 16
PUHLMANN, Anna Catharina Friederica 121 Friedrich Carl Bartholomaeus 125 Pvt 121 125
PULZOR, Anna Sibylla 138
RAEBELS, Gottlieb 69
RAMHORST, Catherina Margaretha 115 Friedrich 115 Johann Georg Friederich 126 Pvt 126
RAUSCHENPLAT, 115-119 125-126 128 Christian Friedrich Johann Ludolf Aug 112 Johann Georg Heinrich 112
REICHHARD, Eva Catharina Sophia 31 Johann Henrich 31
REINHARDT, Friederich 86
REISS, Elisabeth 143
RESTEL, Sophie Wilhelmina 113
REUTER, Andreas 105
REYERS, Anna Catharina 33 Anna Maria 33 Georg Henrich 33
RHEIDER, Andreas 44 Barbara 44
RIEHL, Anna Martha 14 Conrad 14
RIEL, Anna Catherina 14 Marie Catherina 21
RIMMEL, Anna Martha 15
RINCKS, Margaretha Barbara 47
RINKLER, Heinrich 73
RITBERG, Anna Catherina 13
RITBERGER, Anna Catharina 42

RIVERIN, Marie 116
ROEHRS, Anna Sophia Elisabeth 119 Johann Christian Friederich 109 Johann Christian Friederich 130 Melchoir 119 Pvt 109 130
ROEHRSCHEIT, Anna Dorothea 38-39 Corp 39
ROEM, Anna Catharina 42 Henrich Reinhard 42 54 Martha Elisabeth 42
ROEMER, Henrich Philipp 4 Martha Elisabeth 4 11 Reinhardt 11
ROESE, Henrich 22
ROEWIN, Anna Catherina 118
ROGGE, Carl 123 Carl Michael Philipp 123 Johanna Lena (magdalena) Dorothea 123
ROGGENS, Carl 123 Carl Michael Philipp 123 Johanna Lena (magdalena) Dorothea 123
ROOSEWEL, Elisabeth 20
ROSENHAUER, Anna Regina Elisabeth 139 Elis 139 Georg 139
ROSENSTIEHL, Ludewich 80
ROSENSTIEL, Christina Sophia 116
ROSENTHAL, Margaretha 53
ROTH, Catharina Elisabeth 40 Grenadier 40
RUEHLING, Christian 75
RUETHNER, Eva 138 Johann Mathias Wolfgang 138 Mathias 138
RUFF, Juliana Dorothea 116 Michael 116
RUMMEL, Christian Conrad 47 139 Margaretha Barbara 47 138 Philipp Adam 47
RUNKEL, Capt 95
RUPPORT, Johann Adam 49 Michael 50 Regina 50
SACKERT, Carolina 16 Conrad 16
SADLER, Anna Maria 33
SANDMOELLER, Catharina Elisabeth 26 Friedrich 26
SATTLER, Catharina Maria 129 Catherina Rebecca 119 Corp 129 Heinrich August 119

SCHAEFER, Christiana Margaretha 103
SCHAEFFER, Anna Elisabeth 57 Henrich 57 Martha Elisabeth 57
SCHANZ, Anna Martha 14
SCHECK, Adam 13 Anna Martha 13
SCHEER, Capt 12
SCHEERER, Balthasar 137 Hunigunda Barbara 137 Mar Apolloma 137
SCHEFFER, Anna Elisabeth 5 14 53 53 Catherina Elisabeth 4-5 Col 37 43 Conrad 41 Dorothea Elisabeth 29 Elisabeth Scheffer 54 Johann Henrich 4 Johannes 5 14 42 53 Maria Wilhelmina 42 55 Robert 4 Wilhelm 29 42 Wilhelmina 29 Wilhlem 54-55
SCHELM, Berthold 12 Elisabeth 12
SCHENK, Bernhard 116 Christiana Sophia Elisabeth 126 Christina Sophia 116 Friedrich Christian Gerhardt 129 Gerhard 120 Johann Christian Carl 122 Sgt-maj 122 126 129
SCHEUER, Anna Martha 14
SCHEURL, Anna Rosina 40
SCHICK, Anna Gerdruth 47 Anna Gertruth 19
SCHIEDE, Heinrich 105
SCHLEESTEIN, 34 Capt 30 42 45 51 55
SCHMECK, Adam 6 32 48 Anna Catharina 32 Anna Martha 6 32 49 Johann Adam 11 Johannes 6 48
SCHMID, Anna Maria 48 Caspar 48 Eva Elisabeth 48
SCHMIDT, Anna Catharina Sophia 128 Catherina Cohra 130 Catherina Elisabeth 7 Christian 104 Corp 130 Daniel 81 Dorothea Elisabeth 7 Johann Friedrich 125 Johann Heinrich Hermann 131 Johann Henrich 49 Johann Ludwig 48 Johannes 7 Margaretha Catherina 118 Maria Amelia 48 Maria Catharina 48 Pvt 105 125 128 131 Sophia 115 Wilhelm 118

SCHMIDTIN, Anna Catharina Sophia 105
SCHNALZ, Georg Ernst 137 Johann Georg Friederich 137 Maria Elisabeth Catharina 137
SCHNEIDER, Catharina 14 Johannes 23
SCHOENHOLZ, Wilhelm 75
SCHOTTLER, Peter 94
SCHRAMM, Anna Susanna 141
SCHREIBER, Anna Christina 50
SCHROECK, Catharina Eleanora Carolina 125 Maria Elisabeth 128 Matthaeus 125 Pvt 128
SCHROECKIN, Catharina Eleanore Carolina 104 Pvt 89 104 Sophia Maria Catherina 89
SCHROEDER, Anna Catharina 30 42 55 Anna Catherina 13-14 21 Bernhard 22 Georg 14 21 30 55 Peter 67 Wilhelm 13 42
SCHUCHARD, Adan 13 Anna Martha 13
SCHUCK, Anna Christina 8 37 Johann Paulus 8 Maria Magdalena 8 Sgt 37
SCHUETZ, Anna Maria 40 Catharina Elisabeth 40 Johannes 40 47
SCHULMEYER, Johann 97
SCHULTHEISS, Eva Catharina Sophia 31
SCHULZE, Babosch 118 Christian 118
SCHUMACHER, Gerdruth 52
SCHURPF, Anna Regina 139 Georg Jakob 139
SCHUSSLER, Matthias 74
SCHWARZ, Johann Georg 7
SCHWARZBACH, Anna Catherina 11
SCHWARZBURG, 115 117 119 121-122 125-129 129-131 Capt Prince Of 67-69 71 75-80 85 87-89 91 97-99 103-104 107 109
SCHWEIGEN, Elisabeth 139
SCHWENOHL, Regina Barbara 143
SEHNER, Anna Maria 37
SEHRS, Anna Rebecka 37

SEIDLING, Corp 52 Rosina 52
SEISS, Johanna Catharina 141
SELZAM, Daniel 51
SITTMANN, Wilhelmina 138
SKEENE, Col 116 Miss 116
SPOHR, Conrad 22
SPRINGER, Joseph 83
STACHSOEFEN, Johann Georg
   Wolfgang 138
STAHLBUCK, Jost Heinrich 69
STANGE, Anna Catharina 55
   Catharina Friderica 35 Catharina
   Friederica 55 Catharina Elisabeth
   9 Christoph 35 55 Dorothea
   Elisabeth 9 Peter 9
STANGEN, Friederich 89
STARK, Angelica Dorothea 7
STEINBECK, Anna Catharina 116
   Johann Georg Christoph 116
STEUBER, Catharina Elisabeth 38
STIEGLER, Anna Catharina 140
STIEGLITZ, Johann Jacob 12
STOCKENESEL, Superintendent 143
STOEHR, Nikolaus 140
STROELEIN, Chaplain 132-133 136
   Gregorius Michael 133
SUNDER, Heinrich 71
SUSTMANN, Adam 5 Catherine
   Elisabeth 5 Johann Adam 21
   Johannes 15 Maria Elis 15 21
TELZ, August Friedrich Sigmund 129
   August Jacob 119 Augusta
   Carolina 119 Johann Friedrich 119
   130
THIEL, Anna Christina 37 Anna
   Maria 37 Georg 37
THIELE, Christian 98 Gottfried 77
THIEM, Tobias 76
THOMAS, Christoph 23
THOMSON, Friedrich Henrich 38 Mr
   38 Sally 38
THUDEN, Ludewich 77
TIARKS, Christoph 75
TIEZEN, Polly 24
TIMME, Christoph 83
TIPPEL, Dorothea Elisabeth 45
TOERFELS, Corp 16 Leonora Luisa
   16

TRAUCHE, Catherina Margaretha
   115 Sgt-maj 115-116
TRAUTWEIN, Annette Luzie
   Margaretha 44 Johannes 44
TRINKETRUG, Barbara Elisabeth 41
   Gerhard 41
TRIPS, Catharina Margaretha 141
TRISCHMANN, Catharina 14 Paul 13
TRUEMPER, Anna Elisabeth 21
TRUMPF, Abel 7 Anna Catharina 7
   Johann Georg 7
TUCK, Mr 27
ULRICH, Johannes 50 Rosina 52
VALENTIN, Dominicus 143
   Elisabeth 143 Johanna Catharina
   Friederika 143
VALLET, Babosch 118
VANMUELLER, Martha Elisabeth 42
VASSE, Heinrich 85
VENATOR, Justus Friedrich 38
VIEMANN, Anna Catharina 29 49
   Anna Catharina 6 12 15 25
VILLGRAFF, Anna Gertruth 19
   Erhard 19
VILMAR, Pastor 11
VINLINSING, 38
VOELKER, Conrad 118 Dorothea
   Magdalene 118
VOGELER, Johannes 30
VOGELEY, Martha Catharina 51
VOGT, Bernhard 27 Christina Sophia
   27 Jacob 27
VOIT, 136
VOLHARS, Anna Martha 13
VOLLHARDT, Anna Gerdrut 120 Lt
   Col 120 Ludewig 120
VOLLRATH, Michael 88
VONALTEN-BOCKUM, Capt 56
VONALTENBOCKEN, Capt 36
VONALTENSTEIN, Sophia Charlotta
   144
VONBARDELEBEN, Johann Henrich
   3
VONBISCHHAUSEN, Col 39
VONBOSE, 39-41 41
VONBUENAU, 30 44
VONDERHEYDE, Hedwig 140
   Moritz Wilhelm 134 140

VONDITHFURTH, 32
VONDONOP, 4-5 7-11 13 15 18-21 23-28 30 32-35 38 40-42 44 48-49 51 53-55 58 Capt 50 Col 16
VONEBENAUER, Lt 38
VONELLRODT, Christian Philipp 137 Maj 138
VONEWALD, Capt 9
VONGALL, 24 Capt 9 40 Philipp Wilhelm 8
VONGOSE, 6 Col 5 11 13-15 42 David Ephraim 15 Maj 45 Maj Gen 25 29 35 Maj Gen Baron 53
VONHANSTEIN, Ludwig August 17
VONHEISTER, Leopold 7 Lt Gen 11
VONHERINGEN, Lt 99
VONHEYMEL, Col 20
VONHUYN, 57
VONKNYPHAUSEN, 11 24 Lt Gen 53
VONKUTZLEBEN, 5 10 33-34 Capt 13-15 Maj 12 18 25 28-29 49 53
VONLENGERCKE, Col 55
VONLENGERCKS, Col 29
VONLENGERCLE, 23
VONLINSING, 8 19 39-40 46-47
VONLOEWEN, Stein Wilhelm 18
VONLOEWENSTEIN, 50
VONLOOS, Col 17
VONLOSSBERG, 17-18 36-37 43 56-57 Friedrich Wilhelm 19 Young 26 30-31 33
VONMALLET, Capt 39-40 46 57
VONMINNEGERODE, 7 22
VONMIRBACH, 57
VONMUENCHHAUSEN, Col 12
VONPOELLNITZ, Augusta Carolina 119 Friedrich August 120
VONPRUESCHENCK, Col 52
VONRAUSCHENPLAT, Brig 108 Col 66 68-69 73-75 78 83 86 89 103 105 107 Maj 68 71 77-78 80-83 85 94 96-97 Sgt-maj 95
VONRAUSCHERNPLAT, Col 75
VONROEDER, Capt 47 Friedrich Wilhelm 138
VONROTH, Sophia Charlotta 144

VONSCHOELL, Capt 123 Carl Friederich 123
VONSTEIN, Capt 22
VONTRUEMBACH, 12
VONVOIT, 133 142-143 Col 137-138
VONWALDENFEL, Capt 47
VONWALDENFELS, Christop Friedrich 38 Christoph Friedrich Joseph 140 Esther Harriette Catharina 140 Sarah 140
VONWANGENHEIM, Friedrich Adam Julius 10
VONWEITERSHAUSEN, Capt 15 Friedrich Karl 6
VONWIETERSHEIM, 120 Capt 67 69-70 77 79 85 87-89 91 94-95 98-100
VONWILMOWSKY, Capt 56
VONWURMB, 51 Col 48 Ernst Friedrich Wilhelm 139 Lt Col 52 Maj 30 42 48 52 55
VONZAWADSKY, Johann Georg Wilhelm 76
WACH, Capt 16 39
WACKER, Corp 16 Martha 16
WAGENER, Gottfried 88
WAGNER, Chaplain 137-138 Johann Christoph 136 Johann Georg 53
WAHL, Anna Martha 14 Johannes 14
WALTENBERG, Capt 12
WALTHER, Maria Margaretha 143 Mathias 143 Regina Barbara 143
WEBER, Anna Elisabeth 14 David 130 Georg 22 Henrich Sr 23 Johann Georg 142 Johann Ludwig 142 Maria Sophia 130 Regina 142
WEGESSER, Johann 108
WEIDEMANN, Pastor 12
WEINBERGER, Corp 143 Maria Margaretha 143
WEISE, Anton 39 Elisabeth 39 Johann Christian Friedrich 39
WEISING, Jost Henrich 12
WELL, Christian 22 Elisabeth 17
WENDEROTH, Anna Catherina 23
WENDT, Friederich 91
WENIG, Philipp Adam 47

WENTZEL, Daniel 78 Friederich 78
WENTZELIN, Margaretha 78
WENZEL, Christian 76 Daniel 76
   Johann Christian Heinrich 121 Pvt
   121
WERNER, Anna Catharina 31 Johann
   31
WERNERT, Anna Martha 15 Henrich
   15
WETZLER, Carolina 16
WEYH, Anna Regina 140
WICKS, Anna Maria 49 Dorothea
   Christina 49 Johann Christoph 49
WIEDERHOLD, Maria Elisabeth 5 15
   21 Reinhard 15
WIEGANDT, Anna Martha 41
WIELTECK, Fredrica Heinerica 9
   Johann George 9 Joseph Carl 9
WIETERSHEIM, 117 123-124 126
   130 Capt 80
WILDSCHECK, Helena Henrika 142
   Johann Friederich 142 Joseph Carl
   142
WILLE, Johann Julius George 122 Pvt
   122
WINTER, Marion 142 Martin 117
   Sophia 117
WIPLING, Cannoneer 130 Georg 82
   Johann August 109 Widow 109
WIRTH, Gertruth 10 Johann Friedrich
   10 Peter Paul 10
WIRTHS, Gerdruth 52 Peter Paul 52
   Rosina 52
WITTGENSTEIN, Count 125
WOLF, Philip 127 Philipp 122 Sophia
   Philippine 127 Susanna Elisabeth
   122
WOLFF, Anna Regina 140 Friederich
   Benjamin Carl Hero 128 Henrich
   14 Johann Martin 140 Tobias 140
WREDE, Capt 37
WUNDER, Anna Sophia Elisabeth
   119
WUNDERLICH, Margaretha 139
ZEHR, Burghard 24
ZELAZIN, Gertruth Sophie 13
ZERTZ, Elisabeth 29 Johannes 29
ZUELCH, Adam 44

www.ingramcontent.com/pod-product-compliance
Lightning Source LLC
Chambersburg PA
CBHW071426160426
43195CB00013B/1824